Beyond the Ranks

Jose Castro

Published by Jose Castro, 2023.

Beyond the Ranks: A Mustang Officer's Leadership Notes They Don't Teach in School

Copyright © 2023 Jose Castro

All rights reserved.

Published by Jose Castro

Reston, Virginia

First edition

Printed in the United States of America

Disclaimer: The views and opinions expressed in this book are those of the author and do not necessarily reflect the official policy or position of the Department of Defense and the government of the United States. Any content related to government practices, policies, or procedures is based on the author's own experience, and should not be construed as an official statement.

For permissions, contact the author at:

jc@valcraftco.com

Table of Contents

<u>Dedication</u>

I dedicated this book to the cherished memory of my grandmother. I'll never forget the years I lived with her. She never learned to drive and perhaps did not go beyond fifth grade, but her hard work, kindness, grace, unconditional love, faith, and prayers propelled me farther than I ever imagined.

<u>Special Thanks</u>

I would like to extend my heartfelt thanks to my dear friend, Ben, for his invaluable feedback and support through the writing process. His wisdom has truly enriched my life since we met serving overseas together.

PREFACE

As a kid and teenager, I sought quotes from celebrated leaders, thinking it would prepare me for life. It did, like I never imagined. I loved sharing quotes and lessons with close friends who also aspired to fulfill their dreams. As an adult, advancing in my career, my passion for discovering wisdom and sharing it continued to grow. My goal is to empower others to navigate life's challenges, achieve their aspirations, and create lasting fulfillment. That is why I wrote this book, to share what I've learned, in the hope that it helps you achieve your dreams and find a profoundly meaningful path in your journey.

This book is for all professionals. It is for those who hunger for knowledge on how to become more effective managers, better leaders, and strategic planners seeking a fulfilling career. If you've ever desired guidance and mentorship, only to discover that the road to leadership does not have many who are willing to share their wisdom with you, this book can be your companion you can quickly reference. It is not a book just for junior professionals. As I've advised my senior leaders and seen them implement the tools I've shared, I can say that there are lessons here that can also benefit professionals who are seasoned leaders and managers. The lessons in this book will equip professionals who want to be in leadership jobs for the right reasons. To serve.

Why "Beyond the Ranks"? Because leadership principles transcend the military, industry, and any systems of organizational rules and constraints much like the rules on a chess board. What is a Mustang Officer? A Mustang Officer is a military officer who previously served as an enlisted service member before earning a commission as an officer. Mustang officers bring a different perspective to their roles, as they have firsthand experienced life as enlisted personnel. This background can provide Mustang Officers with valuable insights and deep understanding of leadership challenges.

I enlisted in the Air Force more than 20 years ago. After a few years of serving as an enlisted member of the Air Force, I started a program to commission as a second lieutenant (O-1). The first difficult lesson I discovered was that I was not a born leader. As much as I wanted to be a leader, the path to becoming an effective leader was often foggy because of a lack of mentorship. Perhaps you've also observed a limited number of senior leaders who are willing to share the tools of the trade. It can feel like you don't fit in or if you are navigating alone. A frustration I faced was that the guidance that was offered through leadership training would fall short of what I needed to become a better leader. A few friends and I agree that we learned so much more from each other than from what the Air Force was teaching us. In fact, we've shared the idea that in order to be strong leaders, we've had to unlearn some of the nonsense we learned in some leadership training.

Browsing the internet, a while back, the picture below came up. It is a picture of a dog holding its own leash and going for a walk. It reflected how I felt at times about mentorship in the Air Force. You need to pick up your own leash and keep walking forward. Forge a path forward. As I advanced in rank, the junior officers working with me echoed these sentiments. No one had taught them how to do their job more efficiently and more effectively.

What frustrated me more is that a couple of these young officers I met had served directly under senior leaders as executive officers (i.g., Aide de Camp, executive assistant), but no one had taken the time to show them some tools of the trade that they could employ to be better managers and leaders.

They had served directly under leaders who had been considered perhaps the most effective officers among their peers, yet they never taught their immediate subordinates anything.

It was not always foggy. From time to time, I was extremely blessed to find a few great leaders along the way who were willing to share some wisdom with me. It made a big difference. I share some of their wisdom here in this book.

I have experienced some tough failures, but I've also enjoyed some great wins. My hope is that the lessons in this book will help you go faster and farther than I did. My prayer is that you don't experience the pitfalls I did.

These lessons extend beyond military service. While some are tailored for military leaders, the core principles are universally applicable to civilian career paths. Leadership knows no boundaries and these lessons will help you in any arena. This book could help ignite your career. With strong values and lessons here, your imagination will be your limit.

This book is not a critique of broken promotion systems. I'm not going to try to fix the system. What I can do is help you be a better leader and hope that others in leadership positions who will come across this book will be inspired to do the same for those around them. Maybe we can see enough growth in our professional communities that we won't let "the system" get in the way of where we decide to go with our careers and how we help others achieve their dreams.

My desire is that you experience an enriched life of service, leaving an indelible mark of blessings on the lives of those who work closely with you. This is the greatest gift you can offer them, and it is the greatest gift that you can take with you. That will define who you really are. It won't be your rank at retirement or your last job in the military. Ranks and promotions are subject to the quirks of a flawed system, but the essence of your leadership, the values you stand by, the compassion you have toward others, and the trust you create are lasting treasures that will reflect who you really are.

INTRODUCTION

To help you navigate through the book, this book has four main sections: Personal Effectiveness, Leadership Notes, Management Notes, and Career Planning. They are all essential to making you a well-rounded leader.

The Personnel Effectiveness section will help you become more efficient and impactful as a young professional. It will help you embrace the challenges of today's world, grow your skills in the art of leadership, and offer you a greater perspective on how you can thrive in life and your career. This section will help you "Bloom where you are planted", lead with purpose, and navigate a volatile landscape of personal and professional challenges.

In the "Leadership Notes" section, you will discover wisdom and practical advice for fostering a positive team culture, making impactful decisions, building trust, having candor, and handling mistakes with grace.

In the "Management Notes" Section, the lessons will help you in hiring the right talent, setting and tracking clear priorities, maintaining unity of command, and more tools essential for strong management.

In the "Navigating Your Career Path" section, you will find lessons in finding meaning in your professional journey. It will help you set key decision points for your career and recognize the true measure of success.

I sequenced these topics in this order because if you want to pursue a leadership journey, you need to work on yourself first. You need to be effective on your own. Then you need to learn leadership skills and be an effective manager. Finally, you need to chart your course for the career path that you want.

Full disclosure, I used AI to help edit a couple sections in this book to test and confirm that I was conveying the message I wanted to share. You will see that these lessons come from personal experiences. These are not lessons that schools or AI can or will teach you.

Also, I'll share a disclaimer. I'm not an academic. I'm positive that there are officers who could have written this in a much more polished fashion than me.

Finally, I am a Christian, albeit a terribly flawed one. Although you'll find a couple lessons here that include Christian beliefs and you don't consider them as facts, you can still find some truth. Regardless of your beliefs, I invite you to read all the lessons in this book, for they contain valuable insights that apply in everyone's leadership journey. Let the universal wisdom here equip you in your unique path.

PERSONAL EFFECTIVENESS NOTES

1. "<u>Those who know 'how' will always have a job. Those who know 'why' will be their bosses.</u>" (Emmerson)

Learn how to do your job as best you can, but also learn why.

It is a sad sight to see young troops ask me to fill out a form without knowing why that form needs to be filled out.

Teach your troops how to do their jobs but teach them why. Help them grow to be leaders. Don't just tell them to go do something. Explain the impact, the why, and how they fit in the larger organization.

If you don't understand the "why" of your current tasks, you need to find a way to get some "tutoring", either from your boss or your team. Don't be afraid to ask, especially if you just got to your unit. I remember having to ask when I was brand new at a unit. I said, "I'm not dumb, I'm just new. Help me understand the 'why' of what we are doing."

If your boss is making a decision and you don't understand why, ask, "Can we use this as a teaching moment? For my edification, can you share why you're deciding that?"

2. "<u>With great power comes great ignorance.</u>"

When I first heard this quote, it resonated with me because of what an Army First Sergeant (E-8) had taught me; the more you advance in rank, the more ignorant you will be about what happens in the front line. And you're not any smarter than the day before you pinned on or sewed on your new rank. You must establish solid tools, rules of engagement, and a battle rhythm that ensures you have the latest ground truth. Most importantly, you also need to create an environment where people are comfortable sharing the truth with you.

Never underestimate the "spin" factor. I would write status reports as a Captain (O-3) and by the time it was edited to be presented to the Senior Executive Service (SES) civilian, the report had a lot of words, but it did not say anything! It was "vanilla." An SES civilian is an executive level position equivalent to a general or flag officer in the military and akin to C-suite level leaders in the private sector. If you are the senior leader, you will need to grow the relationship between your front-line leaders and you so that you are afforded "ground truth" in a timely manner without any mid-level manager putting some spin on it before getting to you.

Something else to keep in mind is that professionals who grow as leaders are usually pretty confident and it exudes in how they carry themselves and how they talk, but it may limit how others would like to share their ideas. When those leaders say something, there may be people in the crowd who have a better idea or a valid concern, but they don't say anything because they think, "They look pretty confident so they must know what they're doing. Why would I say anything?"

The truth is that we don't know it all. Create an environment where your team feels comfortable piping up and sharing their thoughts and ideas. Ask the questions, "Team, I don't know everything. Am I missing something? Any ideas? Any feedback? Any concerns?"

After advancing in rank a little, I was the one who needed to look out for the spin. I did not expect it to happen so soon, at the rank of Major (O-4), but it did happen, and I won't forget the meeting where it took place. I asked a couple of folks who were supporting me to call in all the project managers so we could discuss a couple Courses of Action (COAs) we could employ toward an issue. I added that I was going to be running late, but that they could start without me and that I would get there. I made it to the meeting. After it ended, I told an engineer who was there, "That meeting went well." He said, "No it didn't! Those people had been complaining for a long time in the meeting before you got here. Once you walked in, they stopped talking and just said 'yes' without speaking their mind and without really understanding the intent of your direction. They just ended up saying what they thought you wanted to hear." It was my turn to find ways to get to ground truth.

Another way leaders can develop ignorance is when they think they've reached a high enough rank or years of experience to where they no longer ask for advice. We constantly tell junior officers (i.e., Company Grade Officers (CGOs)) to seek out senior enlisted members so they can teach them the ropes and to get advice. Once those CGOs become more senior (i.e., Field Grade Officers (FGOs)), many think they know it all and there is no need to seek advice. Their decisions sometimes reflect it. Getting one more stripe or the next shiny new rank does not make you a day smarter than you were before.

Bottomline, the more you advance in rank and title, the more you need to work on getting ground truth and sound advice.

3. "Allow your subordinates to assess and regroup."

Malcom Gladwell, in his book "Blink", shares a lesson from Lt. Gen. Paul Van Riper about affording your subordinate leaders some time to assess and regroup after an attack before having to report back to you.

Lt. Gen. Van Riper's lesson is that after an intense engagement, soldiers and leaders may need a brief period to collect their thoughts, assess the situation, and regain their posture. This is essential for their ability to go through effective decision-making.

At some point, the crap can hit the fan. Give your subordinate team leaders the time to assess, regroup, and to brief you on their approach. Let them fix it without you freaking out about a problem. Offer them support.

Otherwise, you will either get inaccurate assessments, poor plans, and eventually a crop of junior leaders who don't want to share anything with you.

4. "If you cannot explain it to a child, you don't understand it well enough." (Albert Einstein)

Develop the skill to break down complex issues and to explain them in an understandable manner to other people. I've known some engineers and physicists who could talk to me about math that could make you pass out and wake up bewildered in a cold sweat. But the key is to be a professional who can also translate those matters to people who do not have your background and insight. It takes a greater level of understanding to be able to do this. Lead those folks through a better understanding of the matter at hand and see to it that they have that "aha moment."

If you can succinctly explain a complex issue without losing context, you will stand out as someone who owns their tradecraft and is smarter than your average bear.

As you go through your career, you will see a truth that Einstein shared about how anyone can know things, but the point is to understand them. If you can understand and be able to help others understand, you will be a more effective leader.

5. "<u>Identify which is the alligator closest to your boat</u>."

When everything is important, support what is more urgent.

We had been running our office like mad trying to work everything that was getting thrown at us. Everything was important. As my boss briefed his boss, it became clear that there were several important things that we needed to get done and we may not have the bandwidth for it. His boss asked, "Which one is the closest alligator to the boat?" and it gave us guidance on how we should prioritize things. Which were the things that were going to affect us first?

6. "<u>Never take counsel of your fears</u>." (Andrew Jackson)

As you start your career, there will be opportunities that can seem so challenging, they will scare you. Throw your fear to the wind and go for it. Take those opportunities.

If you look back at history, some of the people who changed this world started out so young. Do not hesitate because of your age and inexperience. Stay curious and move towards your goals with a sense of urgency.

This lesson also goes for teams. When a team goes through a scandal or a great loss, they develop scar tissue, and they establish a new governance structure that prevents anyone from coming close to committing the same mistakes of the past. The problem is that fear permeates other areas of the organization, and it creates so much atrophy through lots of red tape. It slows everything down.

With fear, organizations lose focus of the right priorities. Don't let your teams take counsel of their fears as well.

7. "<u>Don't look for balance. Look for harmony</u>."

I got this advice from one supervisor who would pause to mentor me and offer tools that would make me a better officer. He shared that there was no such thing as pursuing balance between your work and personal life. You needed to pursue harmony between the two. It reminded me of what another officer I ran into would say. "I can be the best officer, mother, and wife in the world, but not all on the same day." You need to block time for each of your needs; work, children, marriage, etc. Look for ways for you to dedicate a significant amount of time to your family and your work..

A good friend of mine shared that when you schedule those time blocks to have quality time with your family, you cannot schedule slivers of time for each area of your life and think that you have scheduled "quality" time. Looking for quality time is like mining for gold. You need to dedicate a lot of time to find the gold. You can't just schedule it and immediately find the gold. Schedule as much time as you can to spend with your family. Concentrate on that and during your time together, you will find gold.

8. "<u>If no one is going to lose their birthday tomorrow because you do not send that next email, go home and be with your family</u>."

During my staff job, my boss shared this with me. Know when to call it a day. When you look at your schedule and tasks ahead, estimate what can be done. At some point during the day, you need to go home and be with your family. If you don't have a family, you also need the time to take care of yourself. Ask yourself, "If I don't finish sending this email today, will someone lose their birthday tomorrow?" If not, go home.

9. "<u>You can't pour from an empty cup</u>."

This is another lesson in taking care of yourself but offering a different standpoint.

A wise leader I met from private industry shared this with me. She added "You would not give someone a burnt-out candle, but that is exactly what you do when you neglect self-care. You want to give your team and your family the best of you, not what's left of you!"

Take care of yourself! Recharge! Find a hobby and a way to recreate (i.e., re-create) yourself regularly. Get some rest! Do not burn yourself out with work.

You need rest. This is an area where I failed for a long time. It was not until I decided to learn to ride motorcycles, bought a Harley, and rode from Texas to the Grand Canyon that I felt so recharged like I had never felt before. Getting there on the bike and seeing the majesty of the Grand Canyon, Horseshoe Bend, and Monument Valley filled my heart so much. Take some time to take care of yourself.

Get a hobby, especially if you're going through a difficult time because of a loss or a bad experience at work. Anything that will challenge your intellect and your courage is always a good form of therapy.

While you're taking time off, take the opportunity to learn and sharpen your skills. Maxwell tells the story of two men who competed in chopping wood.

One of the men was big and tall while the other one was short. The bigger man thought he had won the competition from the start. As the day went by, the shorter man took a lot of breaks. This made the bigger man more confident. However, at the end of the day, the shorter man won! The reason behind it was that the smaller guy would sharpen his ax while he rested. You need to rest and sharpen your ax.

10. "If you have a good idea, say it in public."

When I started to work on leading software development in the military, I was assigned to an organization where two engineers were competing for a senior engineering job. In that competition, one of them noticed that others would shoot down good ideas because of any personal reason but when it came down to it, they were good ideas that made sense, and would improve the organization. Perhaps it was envy, competition, selfishness, or any other reason, but there had to be a way to share smart ideas. He said, "If we share a smart idea in public, and not just 2 or 3 people in the room, others will hesitate to shoot down smart ideas because only dumb people shoot down smart ideas, and they don't want to look dumb in public." Talk to a trusted friend and share your ideas so they can help you prepare to pitch your ideas to the team. Then share it with the team, in public.

11. "Have a relationship with your counterparts."

It can be common for your organization to do business with another organization, within your enterprise or externally. Identify your counterpart over there and build rapport to create a working relationship. If something comes up, handle it together if needed before it bubbles to the top. Sometimes your troops will run into an issue that you can solve at your level if you have that working relationship with your counterpart.

The best partnerships are successful when each person in the organization has a working relationship with their counterpart in the other organization. I once took over a program where the military chain of command complained about the contractor's performance. I asked if our leaders had ever met the contractor's leadership? They said they had never met them. I advised, "In order for this to work, there must be a regular "how ya doin'?" to get up to date regarding the latest successes and progress of the teams involved.

You cannot lead by contract. A contract is just permission to have a relationship. Once you get legal teams involved in any dispute, you may not even get what you hired a team to do . You cannot lead by remote control. You cannot lead without relationships.

Build a working relationship with your counterparts and help your troops build their relationship with their counterparts.

12. "At some point, all of us need help."

Don't be afraid to ask for help. A quote I read as a kid has always been at the back of my mind, "One hand washes the other." We are here for each other. It is important to know when we need help and to go ahead and ask for it.

We are usually not as good as we think we are and as we work toward our goals, there will be days when we need help to keep going. Seek help. Seek wisdom. Recognizing when we need help is a sign of true strength, reflecting that we understand we can't achieve everything, but that with help we are willing to re-attack a target and achieve our mission.

There have been times I've needed help at work. During my divorce, my attention span was limited and my energy level was lower. I was not very efficient at work during that time. I had to take some time off. The experience of facing such a big failure in something so important in life was crushing me. My team and the deputy branch chief over me were always there for me. I could not have made it without my teammates. They would come to my office to see how I was doing and talk to me. When we were off duty, they would text or call me to see how I was doing. They inspired me so much.

If the type of help you need is counseling, go for it. Do not hesitate. You may need to shop around to find the right counselor who understands your situation and can offer you wisdom you can apply. Do it. Find a counselor to help you through the slump or valley you are going through. There has been a quote I've seen that says, "It is ok to not be ok." You can interpret that in several ways, but my advice is to be ok with getting help. You will come back wiser and stronger. You will also come back with a greater vision for your life.

13. "Be compassionate with yourself!"

If you've experienced a failure, practice self-compassion. Studies have shown that when individuals are compassionate with themselves, it affords them much more room to think and grow. Being too inflexible with ourselves and scolding ourselves locks us into a self-fulfilling prophecy.

A counselor once gave me a recommendation that If I was going through a tough time and perhaps recently experienced a tough failure, to write myself a letter. He said "Write it as if you were addressing a friend, but it is to you. Acknowledge that friend's strengths and give that friend advice. Then read it!"

If you want to achieve great things, you need to have a solid understanding of your weaknesses and your strengths without undervaluing one and exaggerating the other.

Serena Chen wrote a great article on self-compassion in the Harvard Business Review. She reminds us that "when we experience a setback, we either blame others or we blame ourselves. We may even berate ourselves". I have. Still, neither approach is productive. Chen recommends "we treat ourselves as if we would a friend in a similar situation." She points out that "we would be kind, understanding, and encouraging" (Serena Chen).

According to Chen, "people who practice self-compassion also have a better understanding that failures are a shared human experience. They feel bad about their failure, but they don't let their emotions take over." Something that resonated with me is how she explains that "one of the key requirements for self-improvement is having a realistic assessment of where we stand. We must know our strengths and our limitations." She explains that "convincing ourselves that we are better than we are leads to complacency, and thinking we're worse than we are leads to defeatism." Both will hinder our growth. "When people can treat themselves with compassion, they are better able to arrive at a realistic self-assessment, which turns out to be a foundation for improvement. It becomes a foundation for a growth mindset" (Serena Chen).

A few takeaways that I learned from Chen is that Self compassion can lead to growth more than self butt-chewing and that "self-compassion sustains a thought process that establishes that you truly believe in yourself." "You will need to decide between 'self-compassion' vs. 'Self-contempt.'" It is much healthier to decide for self-compassion (Serena Chen).

As it applies to leadership, she says that "self-compassion and compassion for others are linked. Practicing one boosts the other. Being kind and nonjudgmental toward self is a good practice for treating others compassionately." Chen writes that "subordinates can discern when their leaders have growth mindsets, which makes them more motivated and satisfied, not to mention more likely to adopt growth mindsets themselves" (Serena Chen).

Finally, what impressed me the most was the thought that "we must remove the stigma of failure. Failure is a byproduct of innovation...and life" (Serena Chen).

There is an old quote from Teddy Roosevelt called "Man in the Arena." It has always helped me read it when I've faced a setback. Although most people in my circle have read it, I'll include it here so you can read it.

"It is not the critic who counts; not the man who points out how the strong man stumbles, or where the doer of deeds could have done them better. The credit belongs to the man who is actually in the arena, whose face is marred by dust and sweat and blood; who strives valiantly; who errs, who comes short again and again, because there is no effort without error and shortcoming; but who does actually strive to do the deeds; who knows great enthusiasms, the great devotions; who spends himself in a worthy cause; who at the best knows in the end the triumph of high achievement, and who at the worst, if he fails, at least fails while daring greatly, so that his place shall never be with those cold and timid souls who neither know victory nor defeat." (Theodore Roosevelt)

14. "When the eyes leak, the head does not swell."

This quote jumped out at me from an article a few years back. It is ok to show vulnerability. It will not diminish your status as a leader. There are moments in life that are a true kick in the teeth, either for you or someone you love. It is ok to cry. It keeps us humble, and it is a good thing to stay humble.

15. "There is wisdom in a multitude of counsel."

There is no one genius on the topic of leadership. Look for multiple mentors and counselors. I took this lesson from the Bible, and it has proven to be true. I only wish I had been able to find more mentors along my path. Writing this book is my way of sharing with you the wisdom I gathered from the few leaders I got to learn from, along with lessons I learned first-hand.

There isn't one guru on a hill somewhere who knows everything and can guide you all the way toward your goals. In fact, if you have such a counselor who you need to consult before every action, fire them. The value of a counselor and mentor is that they empower you. They help you identify the opportunities and threats along your path as well as the tools you can take with you. As I mentioned before, they empower you. If they don't, get rid of them. If they think they know everything, get rid of those too.

16. "If you consistently work out of your inbox, you will be working on other people's priorities."

When I first heard this quote, it made me think of how I had to keep a quick pace to get through reviewing the mail. As you advance in rank, you will notice that your email inbox gets more cluttered. You need to be able to get through the email as fast as you can. When I got selected to be an executive officer for a year, I was getting a little anxious with how much email I was going to receive, and I did not know how I could go through it all fast enough. Fortunately, the executive officer who was leaving, is a great officer and an awesome human being, who shared some lessons with me on how to burn through email much faster than I had ever done. Microsoft and Gmail have quick steps that will help you go through email faster. Look them up and get familiar with them. The outgoing "exec" shared with me his knowledge on Microsoft Outlook Quick Steps and it changed my life!

I have reached the point where I don't use the mouse that often. I open an email, review it, and either delete it (Ctrl + D) or file it (Ctrl + Shift + [# of the folder where you want to file it]), and then my next email pops up without me having to go click on it in my inbox. You can configure your email to do that through your Email Options menu. Bottomline, you need to get through email as fast as you can.

Organize yourself so you can go faster. It is said that "Organization is the soul of success." Take some time away from the office to brainstorm on how to organize yourself. Don't be that person who always complains about how busy they are. That is a sign that you were hired for a job that you were not prepared for.

The sooner you can be done with answering the mail that truly needs to be answered, the sooner you can get back to the highest priorities for your team.

17. "<u>A wound not felt is a wound not healed</u>." (John Eldredge)

We would often argue about which officers made the best leaders; whether they were the ones who came from the academies, Reserved Officer Training Corps (ROTC), Officer Candidate School (OCS), etc. Sometimes you will hear that prior enlisted (i.e., mustang officers) officers are the best leaders. We found out it was "d. none of the above." It was not their source of commissioning that made an officer a great leader. It was their heart, their family, and those they surrounded themselves with.

There is another side to that coin. The officer may also come with injuries because of the family they came from and the people they've been around. Sometimes we don't even realize it, but we're carrying these invisible injuries. We make the dumbest decisions because of "scar tissue." I've seen the quote "Hurt people hurt people." It is true. It is best to seek healing so that we can help others instead of hurting them. Your team will always remember how you made them feel. You don't want to be the guy they always remember as the dumb jerk.

Be introspective and see if there are wounds and scar tissue that require attention. Seek help to heal so that your decisions become wiser.

18. "<u>Make your brand known</u>."

A coach shared this lesson with me. As you get involved at work and in the community of your organization, make your brand known by your performance. Identify the three words that you would like your leaders, subordinates, and peers to think of when they think of you.

In my case, I continue to strive to reflect my brand; <u>Inspiring</u>, <u>Trustworthy</u>, and <u>Supportive</u>.

a) Inspiring:

- Empowering my team to grow their creativity

- Kind and compassionate leader

b) Trustworthy:

- Disciplined execution

- Transparent

- Decisiveness

- Ethical practices

c) Supportive:

- Respectful

- Fair

- Acknowledge my own mistakes

Share your passions. In my case, they are the following:

a) Growing a team and equipping them to achieve tough goals.

b) Leading the development of technology that is game-changing

c) Working on something that makes a difference in the community, nation, and/ or greater population

You've heard that "it's about who you know" but that's not entirely true. I could walk up to the White House and tell the guards to let me in because I know the president. Technically, it's about who knows you. In the example of me at the White House, does the president know me?

Others will get to know you. Can they trust that you're a professional of the highest caliber? That is when they'll help you open doors of opportunity. Work hard so that others can learn what your brand is by knowing you and how you work.

19. "<u>Great achievement has no road map</u>." (The West Wing)

"The X-Ray is pretty good, and so is penicillin, and neither were discovered with a practical objective in mind...Haydn and Mozart never studied the classics. They couldn't. They invented them." (The West Wing)

Sometimes it is not about discovering a way forward. It is about creating it.

20. "<u>Learn to speak in public</u>."

There is no substitute for a leader to be able to speak to their troops and to senior leaders. The leader must be able to communicate effectively. You cannot lead through email. There must be a spoken word. Even in today's world where many work remotely, you need to be able to speak to your team and your leadership in an articulate and effective manner. Whether in person, or on camera. Sometimes it needs to be in person.

Some of us struggle with public speaking. I did, for a long time. When the Air Force started making me speak in public, I sounded like I was swallowing my tongue. For a moment, I thought, "Perhaps this leadership thing is not for me." When I mentioned it to our detachment commander, he said he had the same problem but had a technique. He explained, "I pretend that I'm an actor and that I need to be someone else while standing there. Pat has left the building, and I'm an actor speaking to an audience." It worked for him!

If you struggle speaking in public, find something to help you out. Try "Toastmasters". Don't get discouraged. Leadership in great part is about your heart, so don't let issues with public speaking get in the way.

21. "<u>Read</u>!"

It is said that "Today's reader is tomorrow's leader." You need to read.

Secretary of Defense and Marine General, Jim Mattis, explains, "If you haven't read hundreds of books, you are functionally illiterate, and you will be incompetent, because your personal experiences alone aren't broad enough to sustain you." Need I say more?

A celebrity business leader said that one of the questions asked in the interviews he has with potential employees is "What was the last book you read?"

It tells him how curious they really are and how much they like to learn. If you want to grow as a leader, you'll need to read, and you will need to continue to learn. If you don't like learning, don't go into the business of being a leader. If you don't have time to pick up a book, use audio books. You can listen to them while cooking or driving. If you miss a part because you focused on something else, then just rewind it, but don't continue life without reading.

Other than reading, it's writing that will help you learn and grow. There is something about writing down your ideas. It facilitates problem solving, self-assessment, generating ideas, memory, and clarity of ideas. You need to read, and don't forget to write!

22. "<u>Bloom where you're planted</u>."

My first assignment as a brand-new officer was to a town that was in the middle of nowhere. It was such a small unit; I didn't feel challenged to grow and was miserable for the first year. The worst part is that I not only hated the place, but I hated the career field the Air Force had locked me down in—Acquisitions.

It was frustrating that the Air Force decided to make military officers be part of a line officer career field that did not require any military leadership because the work did not involve deployments or leadership of troops. In fact, we could start the job without any formal training. If that is the case, why not just have civilians? Why was I there?

I tried leaving the career field to go to the Army, then to an Air Force flight program. Both efforts fell through due to something medical, whether it was my knees or my color vision. I told my functional manager, "How can I be here to test weapon systems for the warfighter if I have never been a warfighter? I had served in Iraq but as an enlisted troop and we had very limited visibility to the operational environment. We just set up camp, filled sandbags, and got shot at, without understanding the environment around us further than knowing that there were bad guys trying to kill us. Deploying as an officer in an operational field, you get more perspective. I told the functional manager, "If you want me to test capabilities for the warfighter, wouldn't I be better at my job if I had the experience as a warfighter?" Without getting into how I disagree with the Air Force's management of the Acquisition military workforce, no one was listening to my plea to get out of the assignment where the Air Force had me.

I read once that when the toughest dudes run into a problem they cannot solve, they call their mother. So, I did. I told my mother, "I don't know why I'm here." My mother, having a Christian background, told me, "Imagine how Noah felt building a ship when it had never flooded before. He could have easily asked himself why he was there and why he was doing such a task that made no sense." Whether you believe the story of Noah's Ark or not, the principle is that there is an opportunity to build and grow something—to bloom, even when you don't see the purpose of why you have been planted there.

After that conversation, I started looking for areas at work where I could "build an ark" and help. Our boss spent his days fixing issues that were not really issues. I wanted to help where it mattered. I also started dedicating more time to improving my fitness. Then I started volunteering at a local church. In a couple months, I had gotten to see great new places, started mountain biking on an awesome trail, got into helping a youth group at a local church, and made a big impact at work.

Focused on growing, I ignored the negative and kept my eyes on opportunities. Looking back, the town where I lived was a giant truck stop in the middle of nowhere in the southwest. That is what the rest of the country can see it as. I see it as an incredible place with scenic views, amazing food, great people, and a strong community of scientists, engineers, and medical professionals. Blooming where you're planted helps see things that others miss. I grew so much, professionally, and spiritually. Out of more than twenty years of military service, that assignment remains one of my favorites.

If you just arrived at your first assignment and feel like it is a dead end for you, focus on learning and growing with anything they put in front of you. Hard work often comes before your leadership is comfortable to give you a job opportunity that is more fulfilling.

Sometimes, hard work still won't lead to another job opportunity. There are lessons in this book that will help you out for those cases. Stick with me.

23. "Don't lead with your rank."

As I delved deeper into the Acquisitions field within the military, I couldn't help but notice, to my chagrin, that it bore less resemblance to the traditional military culture and more to the corporate world. I hated being in a commander's call and looking across the auditorium and seeing 90% of the workforce in civilian clothes. I wanted to be in the military! I was absolutely thrilled when I could leave that world behind and go to an operational unit.

After my operational exchange tour, I came back to Acquisitions with some ops "street cred" but most of the civilians still outranked me. The Acquisition community is top-heavy. It forced me to rely on my character and abilities rather than my rank. One of the worst things that the Air Force did to me, throwing me into the Acquisitions career field, was also one of the best things the Air Force did for me. It felt great to lead by who I am and not by the insignia on my collar. There was no prompt "Yes sir!" when I asked for something like it was typical to hear when I was in an operational unit, but we led change as a team and made a difference. It didn't feed my ego. It fed my soul.

There were moments that were exceedingly frustrating because of so much red tape. In contrast to many organizations where everything is addressed at the lowest level possible, military Acquisitions organizations surface everything to the top. Imagine trying to lead and drive change there. People get nervous when you're dealing with millions of dollars and, in my opinion, we have not done much to create an environment where we can let junior folks do some "yanking and banking" (i.e., maneuvering) on their own. As a junior professional, I felt like I was in a fight and had to coordinate up the chain of command to get approval for every punch I wanted to throw. You're not going to make it. You lose too much efficiency.

There are some Acquisition organizations that have made incredible changes and have empowered their junior professionals. I really do salute them for that. Most of the units I worked with required you to do a lot of "Mother may I". It took a great deal of tact and negotiation to spur progress and bring some change. There were moments when I would have preferred to chew glass.

Grow as much as you can. Sharpen your skills in leadership, negotiation, communication, and other skills you can bring to bear. That will be what will enable you to lead, and it will be so fulfilling to lead with your abilities. Not your rank. In the end, I'm glad I got to experience military Acquisitions. It feels good to know I led as a junior professional because of who I am and not the insignia I was wearing.

If you wear a rank or a title, try to create an environment where you can ignore your rank a little. Lead with your character and your abilities. There is a saying that says, "Be so good that they can't ignore you." Grow to be such a strong professional and leader, even when they want to ignore your rank, they can't ignore YOU.

24. "Passion + perseverance = grit"

There is a great book titled "Grit" where I learned this from. "Grades, standardized test scores, and physical fitness were the worst predictors of success." The best predictor was the individual's grit.

So, if you weren't great at school, don't worry about it. That won't dictate your level of success.

25. "<u>Save and invest wisely</u>."

When we get our first job, we're so tempted to buy that new car, on top of the student loan we may be carrying on. The problem is that if you are concerned about debt, you will not be able to focus as much as you can on your job and mission.

Save and invest your money. Talk to a financial advisor as soon as you get your first paycheck. *Your goal should be for one day to have your money makes more money than you do in your day job*.

26. "<u>Your life partner can have a transformative impact on your life</u>."

Who you marry will have an impact on how you grow as a person and as a professional. You can support each other, or you may affect each other in a negative manner as you both try to achieve your goals and dreams. Bob Woodward asked Colin Powell, "Who was the greatest person you have ever known? Not...a leader, not necessarily, but the inner person. You know, the moral compass, the sense of propriety, the sense of the truth matters. Who is that in all your life?" Powell replied, "It's Alma Powell," his wife. He added, "She was always there for me, and she'd tell me, 'That's not a good idea.' She was usually right."

Unfortunately, in my early 30s, I married someone I was unequally yoked with. We fought about faith, money, and family. It was a huge weight to carry for both of us. It got worse every year because we managed conflict very differently. After seven years, we got divorced. I was 39 years old. We never had kids. As

I turned 40, it was crushing to see that some of my dreams had just vanished into thin air. During that time, I was trying to get an assignment to advance my career. They notified me that I had not been selected for it. It felt like everything was going wrong. As I turned 40, everything I had tried to be successful in (e.g., Family, Finances, Job) was a failure. I felt like a failure. Fortunately, I got back up on my feet. I owe it to eight people who constantly called me or swung by my office to see how I was doing. They gave me advice and encouraged me with great wisdom. A couple of them were people I managed to talk to every day, and sometimes a couple times a day.

Have you ever heard of Dr. John Gottman? Gottman was a mathematician who became a psychologist. He observed a number of couples for a university study. As he detected small hints that would cause the relationship to fail, he forecasted that they would split up or divorce. After several years, they called the couples back and realized that Gottman had been right about 90% of the time on his assessment of whether the couple would stay together or not.

What was it that Gottman had seen in those couples? Gottman teaches "the Four Horsemen of the Relationship Apocalypse." He explains how if there are just minor signs of contempt, criticism, stonewalling, and defensiveness, your relationship is headed towards failure. You cannot have a lasting relationship with one or more of those four issues.

Dr. Gottman also wrote a book called "Eight Dates." The cases he shares in the book are very basic. Essentially, he lists eight things that you and your partner should talk about to have a successful relationship. Talk through these as they can apply to your relationship. You don't need to agree on all eight things, but you need to be ok with where each other is at in those eight things.

Otherwise, you will start to see each other as an adversary and will likely downward spiral. It would be best to discuss these and analyze them before you decide to get engaged, but if you're already married, these can help you with conversations you need to clear the air between you and your spouse. Here is the list of those eight conversations you can have with your partner.

a) Conflict Management; how do each of you respond when you're getting angry?

b) Work & Money; how much time will you dedicate to work? How will you manage spending?

c) Family; what role will each other's family play in your home/relationship?

d) Fun & Adventure; what do each of you do for fun?

e) Personal Growth & Spirituality; how does each one of you grow? What is each's spiritual background?

f) Dreams; what are your dreams?

g) Sex; what do each of you need to have a fulfilled sexual life?

h) Trust & Commitment; what does commitment mean to each of you?

You can look the book up to get a better idea of Gottman's teachings.

If you marry the right person, you will be able to grow together. Some of the best advice I've heard on finding the person you want to marry is to write down the qualities you want in a partner. Then set out in becoming a better version of you, reflecting those qualities. The other advice that resonated with me is to write a letter to your future spouse and tell them what you love about them, what you're grateful for, and how you admire them. It gives you clarity for what you are looking for.

One of the toughest situations I've seen is when a friend decides to leave their career because they want to support their spouse, and their spouse ends up leaving them anyway. Be careful! Don't let go of what you love doing for someone who is not intending to be there for you anyways. If you know that both of you have supported each other and will continue to support each other, that is a different story. It all goes back to finding the right partner.

Before getting married, go to a pre-marriage counselor (by yourself and together). Also, go talk to an attorney for advice on how to best manage your property and finances. Go to an attorney even before you get engaged. If you're in the military, before you get engaged, talk to an attorney at your installation to truly understand what comes into play in a marriage when it comes to finances and other benefits. There are many legal myths out there. Go talk to someone before you make that decision to get engaged.

Once you get married, I recommend going to at least one marriage retreat a year and visiting a marriage counselor once a year just for a checkup.

Try to grow together and learn how to strengthen your relationship. Some of the best advice I've run into about marriage is that it is not 50/50. It is 100/100.

The speaker I was listening to said, "Anyone who tells you to meet them halfway is usually a poor judge of distance." Also, never underestimate how selfish we are. This is why it is important for us to have time together with our spouse, go on a retreat, talk to a counselor—strengthen your relationship. If you have a demanding job, reserve at least one day a week where you don't look at your phone or computer at all so that you can dedicate all 24 hours to your family. Don't dedicate that day to running errands and doing work around the house. Go do something together. Have at least that one day.

**If you're already divorced and must pay any kind of money to your ex or if you just lost an exorbitant sum of money to your ex, do everything in your power to not remain bitter about it. It will poison your life. Take it as an expensive lesson you learned and go work to succeed in achieving your own dreams; create a new life! Never underestimate your creativity and your ability to create a new life for yourself. If you need to go talk to a counselor or mentor in the process, do it! Do what you feel is necessary to get strong again and to create a new vision so that you can achieve your goals and dreams!

27. "Protect your three F's."

Family, Faith, and Fitness.

There is an interview online where a gentleman explains that if his faith does not fit through the door of a new opportunity, it is not an opportunity for him.

If anything, whether it is work or someone you're dating, does not let you bring your family, faith, and fitness, let that opportunity go. As a couple friends have said, "There will be another bus coming by in 15 minutes." In other words, there will be more opportunities coming your way.

28. "If they don't listen to your ideas because you're younger, leave!"

You've heard the saying, "The sky is the limit"... "But there are footprints on the moon." What that really means to me is that your creativity is the limit—not the "sky" or your age, or anything else!

Several people in history were in their twenties when they started doing something that would change the world (e.g., Steve Jobs, Bill Gates). Experience was not a factor. It was curiosity and creativity. You don't see too many people in their forties doing so much because we "know everything" and we've lost our curiosity.

Seriously, your creativity is your limit. If you can imagine it, you can create it. Spend time with your team discussing what you want your world to look like and go about creating it. Turn it into reality.

29. "<u>When you get to your unit and no one offers insight on where you can contribute, look out for the unit's COST</u>."

C = Communication. Who is the unit communicating? Why?

O = Organization. Are we organized to meet that "Why"?

S = Speed. Are we going fast enough? Are we going too fast?

T = Training. Are we ready to train the next team behind us and the new members? Is our training codified somewhere?

When I landed in Afghanistan, the boss told me there really wasn't a job for me. Some of us Air Force guys would deploy by ourselves and fill in a billet somewhere out there. In my case, I had landed where they just didn't see a greater need to keep that billet and I could get sent home early. But I wanted to stay and serve like everyone else there. As I went to the huddles they had, I looked out for communication gaps, organization shortfalls, speed issues, and poor training. Doing some root cause analysis on an issue that was being raised several times in one of the huddles I attended, I learned there was a unit operating in another Area of Operations, miles away from where they were needed. They were not communicating with the right counterparts. They were not communicating with anyone. Going through the COST assessment enabled me to identify the changes we need to make. After sharing my assessment with the boss, I had a job the next day.

If no one points out where you can help out, stay engaged and look for ways where you can provide ideas or put in some muscle that can help the organization be more effective.

30. "<u>Gauge the three P's</u>."

When trying to identify problems and understanding where they are stemming from, there are many tools you can use for your assessments. One of my favorites is using a fishbone diagram but there are more.

A tool I've used is from the show "The Profit"; the three Ps—People, Product, and Processes. As you listen to a problem your team brings you, perhaps you can keep an eye out to see if the issue stems from People, Product, or the Process?

In order to fix these, you can also use something to frame quick solutions. I've used "Tools, Rules, and Battle Rhythm." I've noticed that if I find better tools for my team, establish solid governance (i.e., Rules) or Rules of Engagement, and create a tempo of when to meet and do vector checks (i.e., create or tweak a Battle Rhythm), a number of issues can start getting resolved quickly.

The other tool you can use is the DOTMLPF. It stands for:

Doctrine: How you do business, rules of engagement, and what are the best practices

Organization: How your team is organized

Training: How your team prepares to execute its mission

Materiel: Does your team have the supplies they need?

Leadership: How are leaders prepared to lead the execution of the mission

Personnel: Are there qualified people available?

Facilities: Does your team have the facilities and buildings they need?

You can also use this DOTMLPF as a template to run through when reporting to your leadership.

31. "Be concise."

Senior leaders may have a million things going through their heads and a very tight schedule. The best thing you can do when communicating with them is to do it efficiently in an organized manner. Never send the boss a long email that is 5, 10, or 20 pages long.

Here is a solid template to follow when sending a request for a decision, coordinating for their approval, or informing your boss on anything. You don't need to include the bold sections. Just use them as a guideline to shape your message to the boss.

BOTTOM LINE UP FRONT (BLUF): Articulate the problem statement.

BACKGROUND:
Present the pertinent information; assumptions, facts, and assessments.

DISCUSSION:
Present all potential solutions.
Course of Action 1, Best-case and Worst-case scenarios
Course of Action 2, Best-case and Worst-case scenarios
Course of Action 3, Best-case and Worst-case scenarios

VIEWS OF OTHERS:
Explain how the situation will impact others if it does not change. Share your assessment of how it can impact others as the situation evolves or devolves.

RECOMMENDATIONS:
Give your recommended Course of Action and the coordination required to execute that action (e.g., Sign, Coordinate, Call, etc.)

Note: Don't give your boss Hobson Choices in your options. That is giving your boss options they cannot truly accept.

32. "Refusing to own your mistakes doesn't make you seem more competent; it reveals cowardice, callousness, and untrustworthiness." (Ben Carpenter)

Part of being an adult is being able to own your mistakes. If you made a mistake, acknowledge your shortcomings, and thank your teammates for the feedback. NEVER try to explain the good you did.

When others experience your mistakes, do not try to explain how you did the right thing in one or more instances. Just acknowledge where you came short.

In some leadership training programs, they will place you in very vague situations. Once they evaluate your decisions, they will ask why you made those decisions. They can be more interested in your self-awareness and understanding why you made those decisions than in rating your actual decisions. Are you able to explain why you made certain decisions? If you come up short, can you identify your shortcomings? We love to say, "I'm not perfect", but cannot articulate how it is that we are not perfect. "There is no better test of a man's integrity than his behavior when he is wrong" (Marvin Williams). If you can't think of the mistakes you've made that affected the people around you, it is possible that you have the self-awareness of a rock. If that is the case, please do not go into leadership. At least, not right now. Work on it and you may be better equipped to get into leadership after you grow your introspection skills.

Serving on a team a couple jobs ago, there is a saying we would repeat, "We need to be willing to call the baby 'ugly'. Even if it is our baby." This means that there are things that we may be working on that are so precious to us, that we would never call it 'ugly' or anything negative even if it is affecting our mission. Nonetheless, we need to be able to call ourselves out and make course corrections.

Sometimes you need to be ok with your team calling you "ugly." One of the guys on my team told me, "I need to call you 'ugly' right now." It turned out I had interjected and made a decision that was not the right decision. It affected him and the team. It was so frustrating to see how I had failed him. I shared with him how terrible I felt about my mistake, "I really failed you there, brother. I dorked that up pretty bad." For a moment, it crossed my mind that I could lose his trust. But I never did.

Always be willing to acknowledge your mistakes and your integrity will be a key ingredient for your team's success.

33. "If you can't get them to 'no', you won't get them to 'yes'." (Chris Voss)

Chris Voss shares this lesson in his book "Never Split the Difference." He explains how if you frame your questions so that your counterpart says "No" first, they are more inclined to say "Yes" to what you want. For example, as they share in the Black Swan Group website, use "Is now a bad time to talk?" to replace "Have you got a few minutes to talk?" or "Is now a good time to talk?" The responses you will likely get are "No, what's going on?" or something that reflects their disposition to hear you out, or "I can't talk right now, but can we schedule something later this week?" Voss explains that people get uncomfortable when they feel that you are trying to get themselves to agree. They feel safer when they say "No." According to Voss' Black Swan Group, another question you can use is "Is it a ridiculous idea…?" to replace "Is this a good idea?", "Would you like to do this?", "Does this look like something that would work for you?", or "Would you be willing to…?" They offer another example like using "Are you against…?" to replace "Do you agree?", "Will you…?", "Are you in favor of…?", "Does this look like something that will work for you?"

A great book to read is Chris Voss' "Never Split the Difference."

34. "People change their path to avoid a problem before changing their path to pursue an opportunity."

While discussing the idea of adopting a new business model when it came to contracting new support, I came across this quote and shared it with my teammates. When you're trying to negotiate with others to convince them to come over to your side, you want to help them see the problem that they will face if they continue the path they're currently on. They will jump on another path if they can see a wall ahead on the path they're on. If you can't show them anything negative on the path they're on, even if you show them several great opportunities on another path, people are generally inclined to stay on the path they're on.

35. "If everyone likes you, there is a problem."

Dr. Robert Gates says, "If a leader is not making a t least a few enemies along the way, he must not be doing much."

You cannot please everyone and stay true to your team. Don't sell them out.

36. "Trust has a direct relationship with speed."

Stephen M.R. Covey's book, "The SPEED of Trust; The One Thing that Changes Everything", saved my butt in one of the jobs the Air Force gave me. I was fortunate to have a meet & greet with the deputy chief of the division and he shared "The SPEED of Trust" book with me. I went home and read it over the holidays. Just in time.

The team I was going to be working with kept some distance between each other. It is my view that the contracting team had done business in a way that affected the relationships of folks on the team. Fortunately, when I came on board, we got a new contracting officer who was solid. The rest of the team members were phenomenal professionals, but they just weren't used to working close together.

There was so much bureaucracy, it was nauseating. The team had been behind on schedule every year, the financial performance was "red", and there were other issues.

Through Covey's teachings, you will learn that there are a few things that will degrade or destroy trust; Unkindness, lack of courtesy, conceit, arrogance, defensiveness, and playing the blame game. Of course, lying and not keeping your promises will also cost you. As I share this, I can think of how I've seen leaders practice these things. Their arrogance has been toxic. They even take pride in their defensiveness, in how they can eloquently articulate a strong defense of how they did well. If you practice these things, it will cost you.

I will go through some of the takeaways I got from the book.

A lack of trust in your organization has a cost. Covey says it is a tax on you and your team. Here are the taxes he shares:

a) Redundancy: Unnecessary duplication

b) Bureaucracy: Too many people have to sign off

c) Politics: Individuals use strategy to gain power

d) Disengagement: Minimal effort

c) Turnover: Performers leave

d) Churn: Stakeholders leave, and no one champions the organization

e) Fraud: Flat-out dishonesty

<u>It really begins with you. Here are the things you can start out with to build trust. You will NOT build trust without these being in place.</u>

a) Integrity

Congruency: Acting according to our values

Humility: Concern with what is right; not being right

Courage: Doing the right thing even when it is difficult

b) Intent

Motive: Why you do what you do; care for others

Agenda: Seeking what is good for others

Behavior: Putting your agenda into practice

c) Capabilities:

TASKS:

- Talent

- Attitude

- Skills

- Knowledge

- Style (i.e., your way of doing things. It involves your personality)

d) Results

If results are not there, credibility is lost and so is trust.

Once you have worked on yourself, you will need to consistently practice trust building behaviors. Covey shares 13 of them. You cannot build trust without them.

a) Talk straight

b) Demonstrate respect

c) Create transparency

d) Right your wrongs (Get rid of your defensiveness)

e) Show loyalty

f) Deliver results

g) Get better

h) Confront reality

i) Clarify expectations

j) Practice accountability

k) Listen first

l) Keep commitment

m) Extend trust

<u>If you are able to build yourself up and practice these behaviors, these are the gains that Covey says that your organization will see.</u>

a) Increased value: Leaders will invest in the organization

b) Accelerated growth: People seek to be part of the organization

c) Enhanced innovation: Requires info-sharing

d) Improved collaboration: Support among branches

e) Strong partnering: Working with other agencies

f) Better execution: Results from increased trust

g) Heightened loyalty: Visible in relationships, low turnover

All these points are from "THE Speed of Trust" book, by Stephen M.R. Covey.

There is some introspection that must take place. You must take inventory of your intentions, your character, and your competencies. Can you deliver results without letting ego get in the way? If so, you have some fertile ground to grow trust.

When our team grew trust among each other, our speed grew. Covey shares several examples of deals that have been made, worth a lot of money, just with a handshake; fast, no bureaucracy or longer processes. The difference is that there is trust. It helps you and anyone in the circle to go faster because you trust the people you are working with.

If you want to go fast, grow the trust in your team and with the organizations that support your team. Observe closely where the trust gaps are in your team. For example, one of my teams was divided in an interesting way; the senior leaders did not trust the junior professionals' skills (i.e., Competence) and the junior leaders did not trust the seniors' fairness and intent (i.e., Character). My approach became guiding each of them, focused on those building blocks we were missing (e.g., Skills, Intent, fairness) so we could have all the ingredients we needed to have TRUST!

I strongly recommend Covey's book, "The SPEED of Trust."

One last thing to consider. In reality, your team has a cap. That is their level of "Trust" among each other. If there is no trust, their success will be limited.

37. "<u>Use analogies</u>."

Analogies will help you make your message more personal. If they can be humorous, even better. I've used analogies I've read somewhere or heard while growing up. I once told my engineer that one of the tasks we had been willing to support was just not giving me the impression it had much value added. Perhaps it was the way it was written. I told him, "I get the feeling we're going to deliver something <u>as useful as an ashtray on a bike</u>." He burst into laughter. Later, we re-wrote the description of the tasks and we were able to better prepare to advocate for funds to cover our tasks. Ten years later, he still laughs about that.

One time I had to brief my boss' boss and explain to him that we were doing well in delivering capabilities to the field, but we were not doing well in the administrative work. I explained that we needed more people and added, "Sir, my team <u>is working harder than a rented mule.</u>" One of his chief advisors grew up in the country and was intimately familiar with how my team could have been feeling at that point because of the analogy I used.

Another example I'll share from a friend, whose callsign is "Honda", is "<u>One person soiled their pants so now all of us need to wear diapers</u>." You know exactly what kind of case this analogy refers to.

With a friend of mine who was just getting overwhelmed with the tasks he had before him, I told him, "<u>Don't try to boil the ocean</u>. Focus on the tasks that are going to move the needle towards green on your dashboard." He smiled with relief and agreed that he was trying to take on much more than he should, and that some of it didn't really add value to his mission and team.

Look up analogies and terms you can use to help make your message more personal. If it is funny, it will help you convince others of your point.

The other kind of analogies you can use are short stories. They can be used to share great lessons. One of my personal favorite short stories is of a public transportation office.

A pastor I was listening to a couple years ago shared a story about a public transportation system that received a bunch of complaints about how the buses were not even stopping at several bus stops to allow people to get on the bus. The bus would just scream by. He shared that the Public Transportation Office's response was something to the effect of "If we have to stop, we won't make it back to the terminal on time." Who knows what had happened that this team had set their eyes on making it back in time and forgot their whole purpose—the passengers! The moral of the story is that we focus on achieving goals that are not relevant. Focus on what is relevant.

There are so many analogies you can use to help convey your points to people and connect with them.

38. "The key to progress is having the courage to start before you're ready and trusting yourself to figure it out along the way. Perfectionism slows progress, procrastination kills it."

At several points in my life, I realized that I had kept pushing some goals off to a later date because I needed to get smart on something, first. Then I ran into this quote and saw several examples from my own life that reminded me that the best thing to do is start moving forward. Action! Do not wait for the 100% solution. It may be too late. Sometimes you need to proceed with 80% of the solution, or even less. The caveats I'll share are:

a) Manage your risks as best you can.

b) Don't put your people in harm's way when they don't need to be.

If your team is good, start moving forward on your goal.

Remember that many times "Perfection is the enemy of progress."

39. "A warrior travels light."

I heard this quote from a Navy Seal who was sharing his wisdom on a short video online. It reminded me of a time when our squadron was going to go up a 14,000-foot mountain as a morale event. I loaded up my vest and backpack with gear. I was prepared. As we climbed, the extra weight ended up wearing me out. It slowed me down so much. If I had been able to go up without so much crap, I would have gone up so fast.

The main takeaway is that as you look at everything that your team is doing and the things that your team oversees, take a deeper look to know what you can cut. How can you declutter the team's environment and processes? This reduces the stress on your team. It helps them focus on what is truly important.

Many leaders will ask, "What is it that we need to start doing in order to be successful?" You also need to ask, "What is it that we should stop doing in order to be successful?"

Find ways to declutter. What are the things that you can say "No" to? John C. Maxwell explains that one of the key ingredients to success is knowing what to say "No" to. Scope your workload to concentrate on what is required. Shed everything else. Travel light.

40. "<u>A person who is nice to you, but rude to the waiter, is not a nice person</u>."

I learned this quote more than 20 years ago. Be careful with who you associate with. Some people will use you. Look to associate with people who are kind to everyone, regardless of rank, age, gender, faith, sexual orientation, etc.

Unkind people will use you, hurt you, and potentially lead you to adopt their negative traits more than you imagine.

41. "<u>Stay strong toward your goals by focusing on internal rewards</u>."

While we may like to look at the shiny medal after a race as our reward, the most successful professionals and teams focus on the internal reward. Those could be resiliency, fulfillment, happiness, competence, belief in self, pride, and achievement.

Trying to use other examples, let's use the case of getting fit. Let's consider getting in shape. You can focus on energy, better health, longer lifetime, and improved mental agility. Then think about listing the actions that will help you get there.

With spiritual health goals, your internal rewards can be wisdom, peace, hope, and some benefits to your emotional well-being.

With financial goals, you can focus on having peace of mind, independence, personal growth required to get there, etc.

Focus on internal rewards. It will help you stay strong, putting one foot in front of the other, as you continue to run towards your goals. Learn to appreciate those internal rewards. It will keep you stronger and resilient towards your goals better than external rewards.

42. "If you're not making mistakes, you're not trying."

I read this quote when I was a kid, in a book filled with quotes from celebrated leaders. When one of the great officers I know came to work for me, I told him, "If you're not making mistakes, I'll fire you. Here's why; if you're not making mistakes, you're not really trying, or you are hiding them." My intent was to drive home the message that it was ok to make mistakes. Mistakes are often an investment for growth.

Although I first read this quote when I was a kid, it somehow got erased from my memory when coming into the Air Force, until I became a cadet. Perhaps because during a phase in my career, the need for perfection was stressed so much.

My first semester as a cadet, I did everything I could to avoid demerits. In the Air Force, they issue you demerits in a small form called the "Air Force Form 341" so we call them "341's." At the end of the semester, I had very few 341's.

Then I noticed a couple cadets who were ranked much higher than me; they had way more 341's than me. How the heck were they ranked above me??? Because it is not about the mistakes. It is about the impact you have on your organization. The lesson stuck this time.

As I tried to practice it, I still got nervous. Mistakes bothered me a great deal. When I had to brief the detachment commander and I'd get feedback that perhaps there was a mistake in one of my slides, in my introduction, or anywhere else in my presentation, I was ready to raise my hands up in the air and say, "I'm out!" and give up. It really bugged me.

In a one-on-one meeting with the detachment commander, he mentioned he used to have the same reaction. We laughed about it a little, but he told me about one of the other cadets who would sit down after his briefing and just write down notes on the feedback they gave him from his mistakes. He would say "Thanks" and get back to listening for the next briefing. Meanwhile, I was flipping out on the inside, while sitting at my desk.

I had to learn that it is ok to make mistakes. Don't let your mistakes keep you tied down feeling like a duffel bag. You could find value in making mistakes. Albert Finney's character in "A Good Year" (2006), Uncle Henry, says, "You'll come to see that a man learns nothing from winning. The act of losing, however, can elicit great wisdom. Not least of which is, uh... how much more enjoyable it is to win. It's inevitable to lose now and again." The Danish physicist, Niels Bohr, said, "An expert is a man who has made all the mistakes, which can be made, in a very narrow field." So, when you see some people go up the primrose path, without the pains you may have gone through, remember that you have been granted the opportunity to gain wisdom. If they have never made a mistake, what the heck do they know?

We'll talk more about "Mistakes" later, especially on how to be in a better disposition to acknowledge our mistakes. For now, remember that making mistakes is part of trying to do anything better in life. Don't let them keep you down.

43. "<u>Never lose your bearing</u>."

Along your journey, you could make a big mistake. You'll probably get called in to explain yourself to your boss, your boss' boss, and maybe even your boss' boss' boss', or higher. They're probably going to chew your butt off. Stand up straight without reflecting arrogance. Let your demeanor show respect for those around you and for yourself. Explain how you regret your mistake, show repentance, assertively, but do NOT break your bearing and let anyone make you cower either physically or emotionally.

Show them that you know who you are; someone who has the best of intentions and has the right stuff to make things happen. One mistake will not define you. A mistake will not change the person that you are. You can repent, learn your lesson, get up, and move on to the next thing; and continue to grow.

44. "<u>Use humor!</u>"

A way that leaders gauge the intellect of a junior professional is by observing how the individual can appreciate and create clever, witty, or intellectually engaging humor. It can indicate their level of intellect and mental sharpness. Prepare to give your briefings with a bit of humor.

During a meeting where we were advocating for residual funding to be allocated to our unfunded requirements (also called UFRs), I told the boss we intended to fund our requirements through UFRs and bake sales. The financial manager chuckled, and I noticed he instantly had a better disposition to hear me out. Humor is a way of disarming people and helping folks get to common ground.

An old boss of mine once had to brief his boss on some of the things the directorate was working on. As he started the briefing, he flipped to the second page and told the crowd, "Please follow me in your hymnals on page two." You could hear a few laughs around the room as they perhaps thought of when they were at church. I still use that phrase when I can. Like I said, humor disarms people, and they open up to hearing you out.

Don't use humor that can be perceived as disrespectful. A boss I had, ran into an incoming unit. You could tell they came from a specific part of the country because of their accent. He was able to tell what town they were coming from. When they asked how he knew they were from that certain town, he said, "I recognized the speech impediment." I almost fell out of my chair. It turns out that my boss was from the same area. They all laughed about it. However, if he had not been from that same vicinity, it could have come across as disrespectful. Be creative and use things that will resonate with people.

45. "Understand what logical fallacies are."

It will benefit you greatly to understand what Logical Fallacies are, as you listen to others brief you and as you listen to others brief your leaders. Logical Fallacies are ways that others can present flawed reasoning in an argument to persuade someone.

Here are some of the logical fallacies you will run into at work. Be ready to call them out, respectfully.

Post Hoc Ergo Propter Hoc: "After this, therefore because of it." This is when someone assumes that the first event caused a second event, when there is no evidence connecting the two. For example, if a soccer team wins a game and one of its players says it is because they wore their lucky socks while ignoring other factors.

Red Herring: When someone introduces irrelevant information to distract from the main argument. This has sometimes worked effectively with a prop or visual aid people can put their hands on. Be careful, just because someone shows you a prop, it does not mean it is evidence.

Appeal to Emotion: Using fear, pity, or other motions to sway opinions rather than presenting logical reasoning. For example, a student may appeal to a teacher to grant them a passing grade so they don't get grounded or punished at home.

Ad Populum: When someone tells you that something is the truth because it is so popular. Being popular doesn't mean you're right. An example is when someone says *"Everyone is buying this stock so it must be good"* or *"This church has the most members so its religion must be true."*

Appeal to Ignorance: Arguing that something is true because there is a lack of evidence to prove it to be false. Lack of evidence is not evidence. For example, if someone says that science has not disproved the effectiveness of homeopathic remedies, that means that they must work. The lack of disproof does not mean it proves something.

False Dichotomy (also known as "False Dilemma"): Presenting only two options as if they are the only options when there may be three or more options.

Appeal to Authority: Someone uses the endorsement or authority of someone in a certain field when they are not an expert in the relevant field that is being discussed. Just because someone is a famous actor or a sports athlete, it does not make them a wise political scientist or an economist.

Straw Man: Exaggerating or misrepresenting an opponent's proposition to make it easier to attack. It is easier to attack a weaker argument, even if it is false, than addressing the opposition's actual argument. For example, if someone suggests installing a security system to improve home safety and their spouse or child says, "You want to turn our home into a high-security prison with no freedom", exaggerating and misrepresenting the intent of the original idea.

Ad Hominem: People attack a person making an argument instead of addressing the argument. This is when people discredit the person's character and their credibility instead of the actual arguments the individual is presenting. For example, when a politician attacks their opponent's character and their history instead of speaking to why they disagree with their proposed policies.

46. "Stay away from negative people."

A friend of mine had several bad bosses and he would say, "at least I've learned what not to do." But I have to share, "Don't study the shadows to avoid darkness. Seek the light to find clarity." Instead of being ok with learning what not to do, search for a place that has leaders who will teach you what you can do to grow in your professional life. If your current boss is a negative person, search for your next opportunity to be with a different leader, with a sense of urgency.

Negative people are terrible bosses and they are terrible friends. Albert Einstein said, "Negative people will have a problem for every solution." Negative people will criticize everything and it is so taxing when they have it out for you. Lyndon Johnson and Margaret Thatcher were quoted saying something to the effect of, "If my critics would see me walking on water, they would say it is because I can't swim."

Stay away from negative people. "They could depress a bride on her wedding day." Protect your peace and your future.

47. "<u>Always have your resume ready</u>."

Whether you are in the private or public sector (even if you are in the military), always have an updated resume ready. Opportunities will come up and you can be ready to present your resume for folks to review. Here is a sample template of a resume I've used and seen that has worked well.

First Name MI. Last Name
Phone number - Email

==

OBJECTIVE: What do you want to continue doing or achieve?

SUMMARY OF QUALIFICATIONS: Summarize how your experience up to this point makes you the right candidate for the job.

SKILLS: List the skills that you have and that are relevant for the job you're seeking

DUTY HISTORY

Job Title   **Start Date - End Date**
Organization, Location
- Bullet 1 describing what you did, results, and impact
- Bullet 2 describing what you did, results, and impact
- Bullet 3 describing what you did, results, and impact

Job Title   **Start Date - End Date**
Organization, Location
- Bullet 1 describing what you did, results, and impact
- Bullet 2 describing what you did, results, and impact
- Bullet 3 describing what you did, results, and impact

Job Title   **Start Date - End Date**
Organization, Location
- Bullet 1 describing what you did, results, and impact
- Bullet 2 describing what you did, results, and impact
- Bullet 3 describing what you did, results, and impact

EDUCATION
College degree, school (Year)

TRAINING
Certifications (Year)

AWARDS
Name of the award (Year)

For those supporting the public sector and those in the military, remember to include your rank, career field, and clearance level.

48. "<u>Never give in, never give in, never, never, never, never—in nothing, great or small, large or petty—never give in except to convictions of honour and good sense.</u>" (Winston Churchill)

"You cannot tell from appearances how things will go. Sometimes imagination makes things out far worse than they are; yet without imagination not much can be done. Those people who are imaginative see many more dangers than perhaps exist; certainly many more than will happen; but then they must also pray to be given that extra courage to carry this far-reaching imagination. But for everyone, surely, what we have gone through in this period — I am addressing myself to the School — surely from this period of ten months this is the lesson: never give in, never give in, never, never, never, never-in nothing, great or small, large or petty — never give in except to convictions of honour and good sense." (Winston Churchill)

Growing up, I hate to admit that I was not a good person. My heart was evil. I knew I wanted to be a good man, but believe it or not, I didn't know how; I didn't have the tools. Even at a young age, I had experienced failure in a deep way. My life was not headed in a positive direction and I was losing hope. Joining the Air Force, my life changed; the core values gave me boundaries and a framework by which I could make decisions. Joining the Air Force was a new journey, and it was a journey of redemption.

Although I was on a new path, enlisted in the Air Force, this wild, and sometimes painful, roller coaster we call "life", continued. I still made mistakes, experienced failure, major setbacks, devastating loss, and crushing disappointments.

There were exceedingly dark moments in my life that I felt so helpless and hopeless. It felt like there was nothing in me that would be of value. Nonetheless, I found hope. As a Christian, I believe in a Creator and reminded myself of something a pastor once said, "Your existence was a thought He had, a long time ago. However tall you are, that space you take up in this universe was a thought He had. And there is a plan for you that involves eternity." Perhaps the most amazing story I've ever read is that of the cosmic war between good and evil. There are times that my faith is weakened, but I hold on to that hope that one day this conflict between good and evil will end and that, by grace, we will receive our reward. Never give in.

There are people who have terrible experiences growing up and it still affects them. I'll share something I heard from another pastor, "There are accidental parents, but no accidental children." If you're going through a difficult time, because of what happened at home growing up, never give in. There is a plan that involves eternity for you. Keep the faith, get help, heal your wounds, and never give in.

Whether it is crushing defeat, colossal failures, severe injuries, or devastating loss, never give in. Remember that your existence was a thought our Creator had. If you're tired of so much pain in this world, He has a place in heaven and eternity reserved for us; we just need to keep the faith until that day when this whole conflict between good and evil finally comes to an end.

Never give in. Get the help you need, find healing, get stronger, and get back in the fight!

49. "Live life fiercely."

My buddy, "Honda", shared a quote from a movie that really impressed me. The movie is Secondhand Lions, and the quote is from a part when a bully is trying to take an older gentleman's food. The gentleman pushes the bully's arm away. Then the bully asks him "Who do you think you are?" The older gentleman responds with "I'm Hub McCann. I've fought in two World Wars and countless smaller ones on three continents. I led thousands of men into battle with everything from horses and swords to artillery and tanks. I've seen the headwaters of the Nile, and tribes of natives no white man had ever seen before. I've won and lost a dozen fortunes...and loved only one woman with a passion a flea like you could never begin to understand. That's who I am."

Here's the message I took away from that. Live life to the fullest. Embrace challenges, seek out opportunities, experience adventures, have unyielding passion, grow your strength and resilience, seek wisdom, and be fierce.

Another great quote that reminds me to live fiercely is Churchill's quote, "I like a man who grins when he fights." This applies to everyone. Be bold and be ready for a fight. Chris Matthews said that Lee Atwater once told him, "David is still getting good PR for beating Goliath". Matthews adds, "Don't pick on someone your own size." So, don't just be ready for a fight but be ready to take on the toughest challenges. Don't go to the bar tonight and pick the biggest dude to pick a fight with. It's about taking on the biggest challenges.

Since you're reading this book, it is a sign that you're wanting to grow as a leader. Live life to the fullest. My bet is that you will do great things.

LEADERSHIP NOTES

50. "<u>Be a flock of wild geese</u>."

I saw this illustration of wild geese on a plaque at a squadron I was assigned to when I was a captain (O-3). Geese take turns leading at the front of their flight. Equip your troops to lead in their sphere. As John C. Maxwell says, "Leaders develop leaders." They don't develop followers. He explains that if we want explosive growth, we need to grow leaders. I always tell my team we need to be a flock of geese where we are all equipped to lead each other. If it is a design issue, we need the designer to get up front and lead us through this. If this is a logistical challenge, we need our logistician to get up to the front of the flight and lead us through it. As the main leader, you are there to equip those junior leaders and to give them strategic direction (e.g., South, North, East, West), but let them get us there. Give them some space to lead. If you are not growing your troops to be leaders, you are limiting their professional growth, the impact to the team, and the impact to the organization. Eventually, great people will leave you because they don't just want to get paid to use their hands, they want to use their brains too. Empower them to lead.

You definitely do not want a flock of teammates standing around waiting on you to lead everything. If you do, then you need to get some counseling to heal some deep wounds.

Empower your troops to lead in their sphere and grow a spirit of collaboration. Create a tribe of leaders, experts in their field, who can lead each other.

51. "<u>Culture will eat strategy for breakfast</u>."

"You can have a solid strategy but if your culture is not great, your team will not do well. If you have a mediocre strategy, but a great culture, your team will find a way to do well".

Articulate the values and behaviors you want to see in the team. Share the core principles you will guide the team with. Communicate these regularly. Include your troops in shaping the culture. You will need their help in tearing down deeply ingrained traditions that can hinder your new culture. Give recognition to successes and to those exemplifying your culture. Finally, lead by example.

You need both a great culture and a great strategy but know the impact of each one. If you really want to create lasting change and transform your organization, your community, or even your country, you will need to start with educating your younger generation with a new culture.

52. "Give credit where credit is due."

During our weekly staff meetings, I had a slide that reflected what we valued as a team. It looked something like this:

a) Trust

b) Helping each other

c) Diligence; own it!

d) Initiative

e) Expediency

We would take a moment to review them during our weekly meeting, and I would give kudos to someone I had observed in the last week that had exemplified one, several, or all of these characteristics. Then I handed the microphone to anyone else on the team. More folks started participating in giving someone else kudos. It helped to start building a culture.

53. "Don't send your ducks to eagle school."

In a conference video, I saw John Maxwell explain why we should not send ducks to eagle school. I think he got it from Jim Rohn, a great personal development leader. He explained that "good people are found; no one can change them. They could change themselves if they want to, but you cannot change them". You will kill all your time trying to change them, trying to turn them into eagles. It will save you and your team a great deal of heartache and time to just find good people who already are eagles or want to be eagles.

It is understandable that you want to help change people. You can help people grow if they already have the hunger to grow. People will quickly show you their willingness to be ducks or to be eagles. I've asked the question a few times. Each time, the individual said, "I want to be an eagle." More than once, they turned out to be ducks. If they are the type that you need to string along, let them go. They need to march at a strong pace forward with their own flag. They need to show you initiative, to be able to "hunt" on their own. If they don't, let them go! You cannot care more about their success than they do.

There are places for ducks, but if it is not in your organization, let them go.

54. "<u>Your job is to make your team successful</u>."

I felt a deep lesson when I heard a story of a man who set a record of climbing Everest, but what he was most proud of was not the times he had climbed Everest. It was how many people he helped climb Everest. When you're in a leadership position, you need to care more about others climbing their Everest.

When you get to a new organization, you will sometimes notice that people are not inclined to come see you because they do not want you to get into their business. If I was the boss at the new job, I used a quote from a great officer I served with, "I need to know your business, but I don't want to get into your business." As Dr. Robert Gates puts it, "Micro knowledge is necessary. Micromanagement is not." I foot-stomped that my job was to make them successful. My questions revolved around a central theme, "What is it that you need to be successful?"

I'd ask folks to go grab lunch with me, one-on-one. I would ask them for three things they liked and for three things they did not like about that organization.

At the end of lunch, I had several ideas on what I could work on to help them. When your team sees you work hard and make things happen, they will grow to trust your leadership.

Leadership is about serving. Teddy Roosevelt said, "Those who seek Responsibility before Authority will soon get both. Those who seek Authority before Responsibility, will soon lose both." Focus on serving and fulfilling your responsibility.

55. " 'CFO asks CEO: what happens if we invest in developing our people and they leave us?' 'CEO says: what happens if we don't, and they stay?' "

We usually say that people are the most important thing we have. How much of your schedule is dedicated to people?

Do you invest a portion of your annual budget to send them to training?

Do you spend time with them?

56. "If they don't know how much you care, they won't care how much you know." (John C. Maxwell)

When I graduated from school and received my commission as a second lieutenant (O-1), all of us were excited to go help our peers and our enlisted force. We wanted to make a difference in their lives while taking care of the mission. The reality was that whenever you got to your first assignment, no one cared how much the military had trained you to be a leader. You had to earn their trust. It started by showing those around you that you cared for them. Then your teammates start opening up and they internally agree to learn from you.

I learned this lesson as a cadet right after my ranking had been published. It showed me at the bottom 10% among my peers while we were going through officer training. It was a slap in the face. When I had been enlisted, my leadership had ranked me #1 among 70+ troops of the same tier I was in. Now I was in the bottom 10%. It was such a great blessing that a friend of mine, Trey, noticed my frustration during one of our classes and asked me what was bugging me. After sharing my dilemma, he mentioned "You should look into John C. Maxwell. He has several great leadership books." He specifically recommended "21 Irrefutable Laws of Leadership." As I started to read Maxwell's lessons, this is one that stood out. It changed my life.

Before learning this lesson, my idea of leadership was just getting things done and chewing someone's butt off when they were not doing their job. I cared for those around me and that is how I expressed that I cared so my translation skills were lacking. How could I show my peers that I cared before they could ever care about what I knew? If no one cares to know what you know and what you can do, it is difficult to contribute to a team, especially as a leader.

Develop a relationship with those around you. Be human. As a General (O-10) in the Air Force used to say, "know their story." Do you know the story of the people serving around you? Do you know where they want to be in five years? Are you helping them get there? A question people ask leaders is "What keeps you up at night?" Ask your teammates, "What gets you up in the morning?" Get an understanding of what makes them tick. Show them you care about who they are, where they're headed, and that you will be there for them along the way.

57. "<u>Courage as a leader sometimes means allowing your troops to do things differently than how you would do them but standing next to your people no matter what</u>."

Throughout military units, there are commanders who will ask their troops to do something, but hover over them and/or just completely prescribe the solution they want instead of equipping their troops to come up with a solid solution. Let your troops own their "baby." Equip them, train them, and let them execute without you prescribing everything to them. Certainly, don't pull the work from their hands.

When it comes to briefing the commander, I've seen supervisors make their junior officers and/or enlisted brief the boss so it looks like they are supporting their troops' growth. Yet right in the middle of the brief, their supervisor will stand up to "better explain" the update their troop was supposed to give the boss. You can see the junior professionals feel like they are just there as an ornament. It was all just for show, but that supervisor is not fostering true growth.

Those young professionals should be equipped and empowered to brief their job to the boss' boss. Let them give the briefing without correcting them in front of the boss. If they come short, it is because of you. Make corrections and prepare them better for next time.

I would sometimes give my boss a heads up, "Sir, I'm still growing this young troop but they're ready to give you a good rundown on what they're leading. If there are any issues they cannot speak to, we can talk later and I'll get you any insight you need, but I don't want to steal their thunder during the brief." The boss understood and congratulated me on how I was growing my troops, every time. Of course, my guys were prepared to brief. One time, the whole facility lost power and my young troop did not miss a beat. He continued giving his presentation to the commander until the end. That morning, the boss gave him a small recognition for his excellence in preparing for the briefing.

Equip your people to take charge of their lane and get things done. Do not micro-manage them. That will kill their initiative. You can't run a unit by "Go do's." You can't just use your team's hands. You need to let them use their brains without making them step down because you're scared they will shoot your career in the foot. Empower them and trust them to lead. If you can't trust them, either you leave or they do.

58. "<u>Be kind, but do not be nice</u>."

There was a phase in my career when I was dealing with a lot of trouble at home and at work. As much as I wanted to be nice, I was losing my temper more and at a greater risk of saying something that was ugly enough to damage my career and my life at home. I ended up calling a counselor to help me through that phase and perhaps give me tools to use at home and at work. If you're in this situation as well, go talk to someone who can help you manage your temper. If you get too aggressive and say the wrong thing, "you can't get the crap back into the horse", and it could affect your home and your career, irreversibly. After explaining my frustrations and my challenges, he shared, "the world usually only looks at two ends of a spectrum; 'Passive' or 'Aggressive'. It is a false dichotomy because there is in fact a third option. There is a middle option called 'Assertive'." Be assertive.

Some people are passive, and others are aggressive. Some of us may start on the passive side and end up blowing up and landing on the aggressive side of the spectrum. Seek the middle between those ends of the spectrum—assertiveness. It is speaking the truth with kindness and love.

Be assertive whether you are talking to your subordinates, peers, or your leaders. If you disagree with something, be comfortable in saying, "I'm afraid I disagree with that idea." If you want to understand why they're making such a dumb decision without considering some important points, you can frame your question, "For my edification, can we have a teaching moment here and can you share your rationale?" That way they don't perceive it as if you are questioning their leadership. On one occasion, I asked this to a Colonel (O-6) when I was a Captain (O-3). I genuinely felt lost, not knowing why he was making a decision. When he explained, I realized he was not taking into account some things he should have. I also noticed he was more open to questions as he explained. I took the opportunity to ask if it would be prudent to consider those points I was concerned about. He actually came back to agree with me. He had not considered some of the issues I was tracking but asking him to share his thought process "for my edification" gave me a chance to share my concerns. At the very least, it would have been an educating moment.

Find ways to articulate your views in an assertive manner without being aggressive and rude. Don't be passive either. With your peers or your troops, you may see them trying to test you. I've had to pull some people aside and ask them, "Do we have a problem? My intent is to help." If it has been with a peer, they usually realize that you are not weak, and they don't like confrontation, so they decide to work with you. People don't like it when you can assertively and respectfully confront them on an issue.

After confronting some people, their supervisors have called to explain why they were jerks and to apologize for them. I would have fired them if they were under me, but we fixed whatever issue was in the air between us. You will be amazed how many people you can strike the fear of God into just with assertive and respectful confrontation. They're not used to people calling them out. Especially in the government.

I've had a couple bosses who hated confrontation to the point where we had to suffer because they were not willing to have those assertive conversations with the layer of management between us and them. They shut down. Zero backbone.

If you are the kind of person who has the backbone of a jellyfish, please stay as a part of a staff team, and do not take a leadership job. If you're intelligent, great. Be an expert at something and stay there. Leadership takes courage, selflessness, and assertive conversations.

59. "We all want to be liked."

One of my bosses shared that one of his troops got into trouble for drunk driving. The young troop was truly the best in the squadron. He wanted to help him out so he approached his senior enlisted advisor to ask if there was anything they could do to help the young man out.

The senior enlisted advisor explained that sometimes we want to help someone out because we want to be nice and to be liked by the people we like, but that we need to hold people accountable. Otherwise, the other members of the squadron will perceive that if they can be hard working employees that the commander likes, they can get away with anything.

My old boss acknowledged that his question stemmed from being human, and most of us want to be nice and to be liked. We want to be "the good guy." Focus on the greater team. To preserve the team, you will, from time to time, need to be "the bad guy".

60. "<u>Know the difference between a crime and a mistake</u>."

Your troops will sometimes make big mistakes. Exercise compassion with them. You should always punish a crime but consider giving a little more grace when looking at a mistake. Anyone can chop someone's professional head off. Only a strong leader can extend grace and help that individual get back up. Sometimes it really is best to err on the side of grace.

When it comes to weighing a mistake's disciplinary actions, try to understand the difference between remorse and repentance. Remorse is when a person is sad because they got caught. Repentance is when a person is sad because of the mistake they made and seeks to change. Knowing the difference between those two can help you gauge how much latitude you want to grant someone who has made a mistake.

You can be surprised at how people will grow from that kindness you've extended to them. If they prove to you that they will not learn from their mistakes, then you can walk them out. If lives are at risk, then you definitely need to walk them out sooner.

Teach your team kindness with your example. As the Lonesome Dove character, Gus McRae, said, "When you give a personal lesson in meanness to a critter or a person, don't be surprised if they learn their lesson." It is far better to teach kindness.

Discern when it is best to err on the side of grace and give people a second chance. And even in your punishment, always kindly respect the individual's human dignity. "Gentle in what you do, firm in how you do it." (Buck Brannaman)

Understand the difference between a mistake and a crime so that you can wisely and kindly apply the right solution.

61. "Go into leadership positions because your vision exceeds the resources you have at your current rank."

I remember having the "aha" moment when I first heard this quote. Don't pursue the next rank or title just because of your ego. Have a vision of what you want to do for your team or for your organization.

As you start your career, you will gain depth in your tradecraft and become an expert in your field. That is where you will grow a keen eye for what you want to do to impact your larger professional community, and at some point you will realize that your vision exceeds the resources at your disposal.

This is where you want to continue growing as a leader in your field so you can influence that change that will make a difference in the lives of the people in your field and the mission. In the end, leadership is about serving. Don't ever forget that.

62. "Practice humility. Look for data that does not support your position."

Always have the objective posture to look at information that does not support your position.

Practice humility and acknowledge that you might not always have the best perspective. Imagine yourself as the jerk in the room, meaning that your viewpoint or opinion could be flawed or incomplete but stubbornly advocating for it as the next best thing since the internet. To make well-informed decisions and foster productive discussions, it is critical to actively see information and viewpoints that challenge or contradict your own. I've read that the Wright brothers would have a rule that they needed to be able to argue the other's position before being able to further discuss their different point of view.

Recently, I asked one of our leaders, "I can see a couple circumstances in which I would support and advocate for your viewpoint. Under what circumstances would you say that we should go with my proposed course of action?" He could not respond. This showed me that all he wanted to do was to have his way without looking at practicality and flexibility to empower our leaders who are managing the organization's highest priorities. He was acting like an infant and I'm not at all surprised to see multiple people leaving his organization.

Leaders who only seek to keep their umbrella of authority without being introspective are not great at leading to make a difference. Stay humble. It will help you recognize when your viewpoint may be flawed. That gives you an opportunity to recognize your team and empower them to grow their initiative and creativity. When they get to teach the boss something, it makes their day.

If you think you're always right, you will experience a difficult fall one day and you will be forced to eat some "humble pie".

63. "<u>If you want to become the best at something, you need feedback. You are not allowed to grade your own homework</u>."

When I first read this quote, it was another reminder of the need to be open to feedback and practice humility. When you are in a leadership position, you need to be OK with being called out.

Do not expect a reverence for you just because you're in a leadership job or because you're taking on a high-visibility project. Practice humility and look for feedback.

64. "<u>Feedback is a gift. If someone is giving you feedback, accept it. If you're giving the gift, wrap it up nicely</u>."

This lesson comes from Patrick Lencioni. An engineer who worked for me would tell others that their ideas were stupid. He would say, "All I care about is the facts. I don't care about feelings." If he couldn't stick to the facts without insulting his peers, he didn't just care about the facts; he cared about making sure others felt like crap. Anyone who excuses rudeness is weak and will poison your team. Your best course of action is to get rid of them as soon as possible. Get rid of anyone who cannot give feedback with respect.

How about accepting feedback? When I was a young troop, with one stripe on my sleeve, I got my first feedback session. I worked so hard since I arrived at that assignment. While we knew my boss was racist, he was fair on paper. During the feedback session, he acknowledged everything I had done well, how much I had grown since arriving, my initiative, my hard work, and my tact in communicating with the people who reached out to us for support. I was impressed that he acknowledged all that. Then, he said, "Now we're going to talk about the things you could do better." I thought, "He said what??? What do you mean 'things I could do better'???" I was indignant. After all my hard work, after showing how I was willing to break my back for the team, how did this guy dare suggest that there were things I could do better???" I was fuming as I walked home that evening. Sitting in my room, I was still upset and could not stop thinking about the feedback.

Then I heard this voice in my head, "Jose, you're always telling yourself that you want to be a good man. You say that you want to be an honest man, too. Well, if you're honest, the truth is that you are not perfect so there is room for improvement. Then why not accept the feedback and see it as a fair point where you can grow and improve on?" I thought, "That is right. I'm not perfect. If that guy points out something that I can legitimately work on, even though he's a jerk, I need to acknowledge it and tackle it."

A peace came over my heart that I can't explain. The ability to understand that, while you have good intentions, you are just human and therefore not perfect, will lift an insane weight off your shoulders. You'll experience a breath of fresh air. It will help you receive feedback in a very positive manner.

Something that can help you accept feedback in a positive manner is to dedicate time to do some introspection. Write down your strengths as well as your weaknesses. John C. Maxwell explains that being able to list your weaknesses will help you accept them when someone else tells you about them. You can say, "Thank you, I know. You're right. I've been working on it."

One of the greatest mysteries I've seen is that we read and read a hundred books about self improvement, leadership, and/or financial management, but we don't put into practice a lot of the things we learn. The worst part is that sometimes we preach about those lessons. As the saying goes, "practice what you preach", but we often don't. This is a common issue. There can be a huge chasm between what we say and what we do.

This is why feedback can be so helpful because it can help us see if we're preaching something but not practicing it. If someone brings something like this up, even though they're calling you out, take it. Thank them, apologize if you need to, and show them that you really meant to practice what you preached with a genuine heart. Then go about doing it!

The one person who can deceive you the most, in this world, is you. That is why feedback from genuine friends is such a gift. Accept it and act on it.

65. "If they joke in front of you, they trust you."

The first time I heard this quote was a huge "aha" moment. I realized it was a paradigm shift for many leaders. As you advance in rank, you may notice some people laughing at your jokes more. I've heard a senior leader say more than once, "The more I get promoted, the funnier I get." That does not make you a better leader. They're indulging you because of your rank. In contrast, if they joke in front of you and with you, that reflects that your troops trust you, and that truly is an ingredient for success. You should observe if your team jokes in front of you. As a leader, you need to be in a position of trust with the team you are serving with. If they trust you, they will come to you for leadership.

Your junior professionals on the team will probably not be open to getting close to you and joking in front of you when you first get there. Work towards bridging that gap. One of the issues you will face is the Power Distance Index (PDI). The PDI was first introduced by Geert Hofstede. It is an index that measures how individuals in an organization accept and expect unequal power distribution and structures of hierarchy. The initial hesitation junior professionals may have to get close to you and share anything can be due to the PDI as they may not want to overstep any boundary of the hierarchy. You will do well to reduce the "PDI" by fostering open conversations, creating trusting relationships, ensuring the organization perceives you as an accessible leader, and involving folks in activities in ways that they can feel more part of the fiber that makes up the organization.

It will help you in the long run if you welcome debate and if you don't get bent out of shape if your troops voice that they don't agree with you on something, or even if they call you out. You're human and you will make mistakes. Get over it. If you're going to be in a leadership position, you should be open to anyone calling you out. You need to be open and receptive to constructive criticism. It will help create more transparency and a more cohesive team.

Don't be the leader your troops feel forced to humor. Be the leader your troops feel comfortable joking with.

66. "<u>Organizations promote action officers who get their tasks done. They don't promote leaders</u>."

I first realized this truth when I was up for my promotion to the rank of Major (O-4). During my work with some senior officers, I noticed that a number of them were complete jerks, micromanagers, and did not find the best ways to create collaboration. Others were glory hounds who would leave you in the dark. There were few who stood out as great leaders.

I wish that each organization would promote leaders like voting for their congressional representatives. We don't individually vote on laws. We elect representatives whom we believe possess the judgment and integrity to make informed decisions on our behalf. We trust them to weigh the complexities of the issues at hand and choose the path that aligns with our values and goals. In our organizations, it would be great if we "vote" the same way for the right leaders to be promoted. Instead, we often promote the ones who just blindly follow orders, have great briefing skills, fill out forms with attention to detail, and follow a checklist.

I've met some officers who just blindly follow orders. They get placed on jobs that hinted that they would be on the pipeline to senior leadership jobs. Some of the ones I've met were total jerks. I would not follow them anywhere, yet some have made it to senior ranks. Unfortunately, other than having a solid understanding of their tradecraft, they need other tools in their toolkit—leadership & management—as they continue to get promoted up the ranks. If they lack leadership skills, promoting them will leave an ugly large stain on your legacy. Not to mention, it will not give your organization a strategic advantage to be successful.

There are other cases where there are folks, in leadership positions, who are really nice, they are great at their original profession, great cheerleaders, and develop a great relationship with their subordinates but are terrible managers. They eventually lead their team towards an enormous failure where people are working on a host of unnecessary projects with no administrative rigor. As you grow in your expertise, you must also grow as a leader and as a manager.

Organizations will promote people who lay bricks the fastest. If you are good at doing what you're told, grow your leadership and management skills as well so you're not just a good bricklayer. Work at being a great architect.

Here are some basic things you want to be able to do well to be solid leaders and managers.

<u>Leaders</u>:

a) Create and communicate a compelling vision

b) Inspire your team

c) Take care of your people

d) Resolve conflict

e) Grow your people

f) Recognize and appreciate your team members

<u>Managers</u>:

a) Prioritize, Plan, and Execute objectives

b) Organize your team to be more efficient and effective

c) Know how to take calculated risks

d) Delegate authority to the right people

e) Resource your team for the workload they have

f) Provide the proper training

If you're looking to promote people, look at evidence for the skills listed above. If being a solid leader and manager were a crime, would there be enough evidence to convict them?

If you're trying to grow, make sure you grow in your profession, in your management skills, and your leadership skills. Don't be a one trick pony.

67. "<u>If everyone is moving forward together, then success takes care of itself</u>." (Henry Ford)

A pastor I've followed used to say, "In the story of Noah's ark, the ark had to be a place that did not smell great and it was probably pretty loud, but it was still the safest place to be." The problem is that in our jobs, many want to tear off pieces of the ark (i.e., ship) and build their own ship. They do not want to move forward together. They do not want to be in the same "ark" or "ship" as the other people on the team. They have their own agendas. That will bring the whole organization down.

It can be an ego thing. There are teams and leaders who see something new and without even thinking about it, their behavior screams, "This was not made here so it is not good enough" and they will try to tear your ship down while you're trying to help them get from point A to B.

The best thing you can do to avoid others finding ways to tear your ship down is to include others as you develop your capabilities or product. Build from effective feedback and show that you're thinking of others' challenges as you build up solutions you will deliver soon.

68. "<u>Practice and foster candor.</u>"

There is a great book titled "Radical Candor" that has a great way to explain the pitfalls you may fall into when trying to give feedback. The book has great lessons on how you can manage feedback and foster candor where you work.

There are a series of mistakes we can make when it comes to providing or not providing feedback. You may end up exercising "Ruinous Empathy" if you don't have the backbone to provide feedback. Some may exercise "Manipulative

Insincerity" which only leads to mistrust and will kill any growth. Some professionals can be too aggressive and exercise "Obnoxious Aggression." This will limit the change a team can experience, and it only causes defensiveness. The book explains how the best option is to practice candor where you ask for criticism while offering specific, kind & clear criticism, sincere praise, and adjusting where needed. This leads to creating trust and lasting change.

I once had an engineer working on my team who said they were not happy working with the team we had. The engineer added that they would prefer to work at a division where they had worked before. They mentioned a specific leader they enjoyed working for. I agreed to go talk to our chief engineer to see if there were other projects the individual could go to. All the leaders our chief engineer spoke to said, "NO! We've worked with that engineer before and they are too difficult to work with, and they never get anything done. We don't want to work with that engineer again!"

I got so angry because this engineer had been with the government for many years, but instead of finding a way to provide effective feedback or firing the individual, they had passed on the individual from one division to another. My team was the last one to have that engineer. They were stuck there. By that time, the individual was set in their ways. I moved before I was able to advocate strong enough for the engineer to be my direct report so I could offer more mentoring.

After a year in my next job, I asked about the individual. They are still there. They failed at the last project they were given and now no one knew where they had moved the individual.

When you don't provide effective feedback and create a candid environment, you leave so many issues unresolved and so many members of your team without the right accountability. Having someone on the team who is not held accountable and given appropriate feedback will hurt your team in so many ways. Create an environment where your team and you can have candid conversations.

You should also push for candor with your leaders. I've seen personnel appraisals where an individual's previous supervisors wrote flowery comments of how great the individual is, but never ranked the individual among their peers or supported their career goals. This was "code" for "this person does not need to be promoted." The individual did not know the difference, but I was seasoned enough to know that flowery language means nothing when there is no ranking or rating of the individual. For example, "This is my #1/35 captains". Additionally, the records did not show any qualified and/or quantified impact of their performance. Their records had a lot of fluff, but it set the individual up for potentially getting laid off in a Reduction in Force (RIF). On the other hand, no one ever gave the individual any feedback on where they could improve and truly warrant a good ranking among their peers. I read all the feedback notes they shared with the young officer. Everyone said, "You're doing great!"

There are leaders who will tell you that you're great, but never support your career goals and sometimes even speak negatively of you behind your back. They will pee on your leg and tell you it's raining. If you're not seeing the support you need, go talk to them and ask what you need to do to have their true support. Show them you can handle candor.

69. "<u>You will make mistakes in hiring people. Fire them as soon as you can and help them land on their feet somewhere else</u>."

This is another lesson that relates to acknowledging our mistakes and recognizing where we came short. Experience has shown me that even the best of leaders and interviewers will every now and then hire a bad apple. Don't think you will never make a mistake in hiring. You're human. If you need to fire someone, admit your mistake of hiring them, as quickly as possible, and help them land on their feet somewhere else. Let them go. Start hunting for the right person for that job. Do not let your ego get in the way. Do continue to invest in something that is failing just because you don't want to acknowledge you made a bad decision. Don't do that to your team. The more you allow someone who should not be on the team to stay on the team, the more you are affecting their morale, productivity, and their trust in you.

There is a short video online of Gary Vaynerchuk explaining that sometimes we want to keep the person there because of our ego—we don't want to admit we made a mistake in hiring. Check your ego and go hire the right person for the job.

Sometimes the decision to fire someone will not be clear cut. I had an engineer who was extremely intelligent and very personable. The engineer and their teammate were leading a project for a few months.

Every time they briefed me, they had a great explanation about how they could not make progress because they were tackling a new challenge that had emerged. After a few months, I thought, "At the end of the day, there must be progress and there hasn't been any. It doesn't matter how well they can explain the situation, there is no progress. The engineer needs to go."

After several meetings where I emphasized the need for progress and saw none, I approached engineering leadership and requested the engineer's reassignment. Two days after their departure, the challenges that had surfaced in the last six months disappeared. The other engineer who was part of the effort came back with a solid roadmap and started making progress towards the objective.

Even when someone may give you an intelligent explanation, even if the leader is extremely intelligent, if the team is not getting closer to achieving the objective, you need to replace the leader. Sometimes, I've seen leaders have a really smart story of why they are behind on a project and their boss has no clue that their lie is borderline criminal. If you just hold them accountable to deliver, you don't need to try to assess if their story makes sense or not. It is all about leadership. Either things are getting done or not. Sometimes you will need to fire people who are personable, kind, great to hang out with, and respectful. If they cannot make progress or get things done, you need to let them go. If you keep them there, it is like having a beautiful, comfortable, and really expensive saddle but no horse. You're not going to look smart just sitting on the saddle in an empty field. Anyone passing by will have a laugh.

Another issue I've noticed with leaders is that they don't have the stomach to fire people. Some reference the quote "There is no such thing as bad troops. Only bad leaders." This is not true. There are ineffective team members. A leader must act. It could be that they are ineffective team members. I've had to tell people up front, "If you continue like this, I cannot afford you on the team." Some have been willing to change, others started to look for other jobs.

Always self-assess. It could be that you did not set expectations well enough. It could be that you just picked the wrong person for the wrong job. If they need to go, let them go. Help them land on their feet somewhere else (if they have not committed a crime), but don't let your ego get in the way of firing the people who are ill-suited for the job.

Bottomline, find a way to remove those who do not belong on your team. Protect your team. Protect the mission.

70. "<u>Bureaucracies can force teams to keep the disgruntled and incompetent on the payroll</u>."

In government, if you are not part of a selective unit, higher headquarters, and high-visibility programs like the F-22, F-35, and others of the like, you can easily end up with people who are completely ineffective and have been floating around the government without getting fired. It is not easy to fire someone in the government.

No one is perfect but in government, there are people who will be utterly incompetent and still draw a paycheck. Seeing them, you won't know whether to laugh or cry.

The government makes it difficult to fire government employees. So, what can you do when you run into these employees?

<u>Talk to them to see if there are issues you can address</u>. Sometimes they are seeking an opportunity to have more responsibility but they're going about it the wrong way. Those will respond to mentorship. Ask them "Why are you serving? Why are you here?" Being assertive will go a long way. These conversations can happen in many forms. In one of my jobs, there was one individual who was pretty aggressive with folks from other teams under my purview. The individual took forever to help the people on the team who came over to ask for support. Approaching him, I said, "What's this I hear about you scaring people and giving them all kinds of grief?" The response was, "Sir, they wait until the last minute to give me their requests. They don't involve me in the process. If they did, I could even provide them with a better solution." I asked, "I sense it is because they're scared of you. Do you think you can treat them with kindness? The thing is, I need your experience and your leadership. If others can't come to you because they're scared of you, I can't use your leadership skills and experience. I need for others to be comfortable with coming to you for help so you can lead them to a solution." To the individual's credit, they took great steps to change the situation. They were soon helping the team find solutions that others had not been aware of.

On another occasion, one of my troops told me that the task I was assigning him could not be done. I had been around long enough to know it was possible. He insisted it could not be done. Later in the afternoon, I asked him to come over and chat with me. When he came over, he could see the frustration in my face as I said, "You're the one I trust. If I can't trust you, who am I going to trust!?!?!? I need a solution. Who else can I turn to? Now, you let me know if we need to go to someone else." When a person feels trusted, it is an incredible motivator. He ended up finding a solution.

You never know what the issue may be so go talk to people. See if you can provide a solution, break barriers, or inspire them to lead. Just know that there will be times that the individual may be toxic, and you'll need to start looking for another way to deal with them or hopefully get them out of government.

<u>Talk to their supervisor</u>. You can start a paper trail documenting their ineffectiveness and poor attitude. People usually respond to their supervisor as their paycheck, bonuses, and promotions can depend on it.

<u>Leave them out of the work you are doing</u>. I've been in jobs where I don't have time for the paperwork trail so I will just start leaving them out of everything I'm doing. Your team will appreciate not having to see the negative, disgruntled, and incompetent employee at your meetings. They are a cancer. There was a case where this approach of leaving someone out in the cold triggered the individual into action to contribute to the team. To their credit, they started engaging with a positive attitude. Not too many people like being seen as the one who does not contribute. In one of my jobs, the people who were incompetent and allowed to stay in government were so many, one of my teammates and I had to make two lists to reflect (1) "People Who Get Work Done", and (2) "People Who Create Work." This helped us identify who we need to not invite to our meetings.

Unfortunately, the government is filled with civilians and military who are "Retired On Active Duty" (ROAD) and there is little that their leaders are willing to do in holding them accountable. I've been in units where there are military and civilians who just quit but no one can get rid of them. When there is absolutely no way to get rid of them and your leadership has locked you in with that kind of person who will not work, and you've tried to develop a relationship with them to inspire them, and you've given them projects they fail at, try lesson #91.

If nothing works, go back to your team and tell them that unfortunately that is the current reality you're stuck with. Acknowledge the failed system. Thank them for their character and example. Praise them for their hard work. Reward them. Feed the good grass. Leave the chaff in the wind.

Ideally, our laws and regulations could change so that we had the ability to get rid of people like this more efficiently and thus better serve the taxpayer.

If you are a senior leader, there are ways to reduce the number of disgruntled and incompetent people who stay on your payroll. The healthiest course of action is to create a culture where the disgruntled and incompetent cannot survive. Have a culture that fosters candor, where everyone works hard and provides feedback to those who are not carrying their share of the tasks. If the culture at your tactical team level has an environment where those types of employees cannot have freedom of movement, they will usually leave the organization. I'm afraid that there are times that you just need to find a way to have them fired.

There is one more option which is implementing lesson #91.

71. "<u>None of us is as dumb as all of us</u>."

I first heard this quote at a meeting for Acquisition professionals. It reminded me of Groupthink. Be careful not to fall into Groupthink!!! It is when a group of people have the desire for harmony to a level where they are willing to allow terrible decision-making. Groupthink happens when a team prioritizes consensus over critical assessments of reality.

If you experience or observe any of the following, you may be in a team that has fallen into Groupthink.

a) The group ignores negative feedback, risks, and warnings.

b) The team sees their leaders with moral superiority.

c) Outsiders are seen as enemies and inferior.

d) Members will withhold their true thoughts out of fear and preference to appear united.

e) The leaders apply significant pressure on team members who have nonconforming opinions.

f) Some members may act as gatekeepers who won't allow outsiders to talk to their members.

g) It is perceived that everyone agrees because there is no visible disagreement.

If you want to study examples of Groupthink, there is extensive material online, case studies, articles, etc. Look at examples like the Challenger Space Shuttle launch after engineers expressed concerns about the O-rings in certain temperatures.

A few other examples are the Pearl Harbor Attack and the Vietnam War. Some can identify Groupthink leading to the Financial Crisis of 2007 – 2008. That one, in my opinion, may be harder to study, but the other examples are cases of smaller groups involved in major debacles.

72. "When your boss promises something, do not promise it to your troops."

In one of my jobs, we had a large team that was aware that we had run out of money. My boss' boss told us to hire more people and to burn hot, full steam ahead. He told us to burn through the money because there was more coming for our program that was such a high priority for the Air Force. The intent was to enable the program team to employ more developers as it was in support of operations. He was basing his assessment on a note a senior leader had made on the back of a notes page. There was nothing formal and when we ran out of money, the money that my boss' boss promised never came.

In the meantime, my team knew there was little money left. Most of them were contractors and wanted to know if they needed to start looking for other jobs. I told them, "The colonel (O-6) said he was going to get the money so the money will be here." The money never came, and we had to cut more than half of the team. We went from about 180 people to around 70. I felt so horrible because I had essentially vouched for my boss' boss, and the team believed in me. I let them down. While we all knew that being a contractor does make it a bit more unstable when it comes to keeping a job through the year, I should have told them, "The colonel said he was going to do his rounds to make sure we get the money, but it is not confirmed so there is a possibility that we may not get the money." That is what I should have said, at the very least. The lesson I learned, don't vouch for your boss. It would not be the last time we would be promised something and not see someone deliver. Some people in leadership jobs are politicians and some are "promiticians" who get excited about things so they promise to deliver something to get everyone excited, but they under deliver. They mean well but be prudent; don't vouch for them with others. Just convey the reality of the situation.

73. "<u>Do not play the game of political maneuvering</u>."

I once had a boss who frequently held meetings with various stakeholders across different levels of the chain of command staff, but rarely included our team. As a result, we often found ourselves in the dark, learning about key developments to go in a different direction every time we met with him and only after decisions had been made. This created an atmosphere akin to a soap opera, leaving us feeling disconnected from the decision-making process.

During my time at this assignment, I witnessed a fair amount of political maneuvering, all aimed at securing favored partnerships, while sidelining others. Unfortunately, many of these calculated moves resulted in disappointments. My advice is simple: refrain from scheming and instead focus on decisions that enhance your mission, serve your customers, and support your employees. Rather than overthinking based on the political capital you want to gain, identify the value you seek to create and pursue it earnestly.

In leadership, transparency can be one of your greatest assets. Involve your team where you can. When you prioritize transparency over political games and managing secrets, you will find that your team is not only more productive but also more united, motivated, and equipped to achieve shared goals.

"Instead of trying to do the math, create the chemistry." Grow your relationship with your team, improve your situational decision making with their support, build your team up, empower them to innovate and create, and let them arm you to negotiate through the political landscape outside your organization. Currahee (We stand alone, together)!

74. "<u>Navigate regulations for the good of your team</u>."

Always be ready to stand up assertively and respectfully for what is right.

Sometimes this means you will need to confront senior leaders. There are some leaders who will mindlessly apply the regulations. There are cases where you need to reconsider the applicability of some regulations. If they don't apply, get regulations out of the way and don't force your troops to trip over them. I can't count the times I asked, "There is a difference between a law and a regulation. If it is a regulation, tell me how we get a waiver for it?"

Be an authentically good steward, knowing what regulations are only in the way of your team's path. Don't just mindlessly apply everything in the regulations. Be a good steward. Be ready to waive some rules to provide the appropriate relief to your troop(s) from regulations that place unnecessary hardship on your team. Have the courage to do it and explain it to your leadership. Don't let senior leaders trip over regulation. Stand by your decision. There is a quote I read once that said, "The boss can tell me where to sit, but no one can tell me where to stand." Know when and where to stand for what is a just cause to take care of your troops and the mission.

I have seen it first-hand where commanders will never lift a finger to take care of their troops. Assessing if we need a waiver for a regulation would require them to use their brain and their courage but they're not used to it because they've gotten to where they're at by just blindly following orders. They knew how but never understood why. It makes my blood boil just to remember that we promote these kinds of professionals. They reach field grade officers only to become THE problem.

Standing for what is a just cause, for your troops and your teams, means that there will be times you may need to waive some regulations. Find some courage.

75. "Peace is not the absence of conflict. It is the presence of justice." (Martin Luther King, Jr.)

There will be conflict in your organization. There will be fools who want to have a pissing match with your team or someone on your team. There are going to be people on your team who want to put others down. There will be managers under you who treat their subordinates poorly.

Stand up for your team! Do not look the other way. Promote ethical leadership, cultivate a fair and just work environment, create open channels of communication, and let your team see the results of you fighting for them.

There were a number of times someone on my team came to me about someone outside the team being disrespectful or just saying "No" because they either didn't have the brains, courage, energy, good will, or the authority to say "Yes". I got engaged immediately and left my office ready to break fences. There were other times, a member of my team came to me to share that someone on my own team had been unprofessional, disrespectful, and downright insulting. I dropped what I was doing and my sole focus went to getting the facts of everything that happened. I strived to get all the facts that same day to make a decision by the close of business, if not sooner. These kinds of problems would not be tolerated one more day. My team knew I would be fair and that I would fight for what was right. They knew I worked extremely hard to get them the resources they needed and to make sure they had a work environment where they could work in true peace.

My team knew they didn't need to engage in any fights, whether it was with someone outside our organization or within our organizations. I fought bullies wherever they were at. I also made it very clear that there would be no tolerance for disrespect within the team. I'd say a line from one of my favorite shows, "There ain't no fighting on this ranch. You wanna fight, come fight me." If you know, you know. For those who don't, it is from the show "Yellowstone". I added, "If you want to yell at someone, you come yell at me. I'll lock the door and you can yell as much as you want. I want to understand your frustration and the whole situation. But then, we're going to fix the issue.

In one of our strategic planning offsite meetings, my chief engineer said perhaps one of the kindest things anyone has said to me. She shared with the whole team that in her career she had never seen a leader act so fast, to address the issues their people brought to them, as I did. It was so humbling. It had never crossed my mind that someone would say that, but it was a reminder that your team is watching and that you can make a difference in their lives.

Stand up for your team. If you don't have the courage, don't get into the business of being in a leadership job.

76. "Grow your character."

Leadership requires character. What is character? John C. Maxwell explains it as the set of values you have adopted. It is what you base your decisions on. Have you stopped to think about that list of values you base your decisions on?

As a leader, you will need to grow your character with honorable values; kindness, courage, prudence, temperance, justice, service, and more.

Make your list of values by which you will make your future decisions.

77. "<u>Love</u>."

Yes, you will need to love your team if you want to lead them. You may sometimes need to suffer from cold, heat, hunger, and more, for your teammates. Love, not as an emotion, but as an action and as a principle—that is your duty as a leader.

Years ago, I came across the story of Angus McGilliray, online. It was first shared by Ernest Gordon in his book where he told the true story behind the bridge on the River Kwai.

Angus was a Scottish prisoner of war. The camp had grown terribly cutthroat. Each prisoner was out for himself. They would steal from each other. They each looked out only for their own survival. However, Scottish soldiers, like Angus, took their "battle buddy" system seriously. They called their battle buddy their "mucker."

Angus knew his mucker was dying, but he was not willing to give up on him. Someone had stolen his mucker's blanket. Angus gave him his blanket and told him he had an extra one. When it came time to eat, Angus would give his food to his mucker and made sure he ate it so it could help him recover. He'd let him know that he had extra food.

As Angus' mucker began to recover and appear healthier, Angus collapsed and died. It was later discovered that Angus had died of starvation and exhaustion. Angus never had extra food. He never had an extra blanket. He gave his mucker everything he had.

When the other prisoners learned why Angus died, the camp began to change. They began to focus on their buddies. They collaborated to build their own hospital and church. The place was transformed, because one man gave everything for his friend. Angus transformed that camp. Do you want to transform an organization?

Leadership is about heart. If you don't have it, do not get into the business of leading.

MANAGEMENT NOTES

78. <u>"Hire 10's and 9's. You can use a few 8's, but don't hire 7's and below."</u>

Stephen Schwarzman, in his book, "What it Takes", explained how he rates applicants to decide who he will hire. He uses a scale from 1 to 10 .

10 = They can recognize problems ahead and create solutions

9 = They can't foresee problems ahead but if you share it with them, they can create solutions

8 = They do what they're told

1 to 7 = Do not hire

In your interviews, ask people to tell you about an experience when they recognized a problem ahead and create solutions! They can get really excited telling you about their experience.

NOTE: A good indicator to look for in resumes is if the individual has grown in their career. For example, has the person gone from an apprentice to a technician and then to a supervisor? Some who have stayed stagnant in the same exact job for more than five years is a red flag for me. There are exceptions but I am hesitant to

79. <u>"Don't write letters of recommendation to anyone you have not worked with for at least for 6 months."</u>

This is a lesson I heard from one of my peers in what is now the Space Force. There will be people to ask you for your recommendation. Remember that your name means something. Have a rule that you do not write letters of recommendation for anyone who has not worked with you for at least six months. Writing and signing a letter of recommendation for someone you have not worked with would not even be honest. If they're a soup sandwich at work, you don't want to put your name on a recommendation letter for them.

I've had to tell one of the troops in the squadron, "I've never worked with you, so there is not much I can put down. I can write about how I've observed you to be very supportive and kind."

On another occasion, I had to tell the individual flat out, "I cannot write a letter of recommendation. I can speak to how respectful and kind you are, but I cannot speak to your effectiveness." I had given him many chances to prove he could bring value to the team, but he was so lost in our conversations. He couldn't find his butt with both hands. He was that lost and clueless. The individual was upset because I was not willing to write a letter of recommendation for him with the verbiage he wanted, but you need to be honest, and you need to preserve your name. "It's your name on the jersey!"

80. "<u>There are four types of officers</u>." (Hammerstein-Equord)

This applies to organizations that are in private industry as well. One of my old bosses shared this with me.

Officers	Lazy	Energetic
Smart	COMMANDERS Smart enough to know what needs to be done. "Lazy" enough to get out of the way so their team can execute.	STAFF OFFICERS Smart enough to know what needs to be done. Energetic enough to get it done.
Dumb	MENIAL TASKS There is a place for them, with simple tasks (e.g., "Guard the door", "Coordinate this form", etc)	FIRE IMMEDIATELY They are energetic and people will perceive they know what they're doing, and these officers will lead others in doing the wrong things at a thousand miles an hour!

I've had bosses who ask me if I can find a project for someone who easily falls into "Dumb" & "Energetic." They've asked me, "Is there a project that is less difficult so they can handle it?"

My response has been, "Sir, the question is, 'is there a project that you are willing to allow them to mess up?'" We gave a new project to an individual who had consistently faced issues in other teams. It was a job with less visibility, more support, and less complexity, and they still messed it up. Use the table above to analyze where you need people to go.

There are situations when it becomes a little foggy. Some people are dumb and energetic, but they speak with so much confidence, people believe them. They are able to speak with buzz words or any other words that impress their listeners. In that instance, no one can immediately notice they are dumb and energetic. "Never confuse enthusiasm with capability" (General Hugh Shelton). A friend of mine used to say, "You can go 1,000 Miles Per Hour, in the wrong direction." Sadly, I've sometimes seen these types of officers climb the ranks. The best thing you can do is fill your processes with transparency and openness so when these dumb & energetic leaders do something that reveals the risk they pose to the team, you have consensus from those involved to hold them accountable.

An issue you will face, at least in government, is that too many people are allowed to stay in as "Dumb & Lazy" and no one can fire them. You may be in a situation where you really need more people who are energetic, and your organization has too many "Dumb & Lazy" floating around. The organization needs to limit how many people are allowed to stay employed while the extent of their God-given skills is doing menial tasks.

A challenge you will see is that, from time to time, we all find ourselves in all the quadrants of the table above. The key is to stay consistently in the quadrant where our team needs us. There was a moment where my deputy had to tell me, "Sir, get out of the way" because I was the guy in charge, and I was acting like a staff officer. Another time, he said "Remember that if you share an idea with the team, they will see it as an order. Let's discuss it first." I had to get out of the way and use his experience to shape our future instead of acting like a staff officer and getting right in the middle of the team's path.

81. "<u>Know the difference between a risk and an issue</u>."

As you kick off any undertaking, assess what your issues are and what your risks are. If there aren't any, be careful you may not be going in with all the intel you should have.

An issue is something that has already occurred or is currently happening, and you can address it. A risk is a potential future event. Risks are uncertain. You will need to determine a strategy to manage risk. You will need to pick a strategy from the following:

a) Mitigate: Take proactive steps to reduce the likelihood and/or impact of a risk.

b) Transfer: Shift responsibility for managing the risk to another party (e.g., purchase insurance)

c) Avoid: Take actions to eliminate the risk entirely by not executing the operation that presents the risk

d) Accept: Consciously not taking any action to mitigate, transfer, or avoid it.

As you analyze things, look into root causes. think "Why do we even have this risk, to begin with?"

One way that will help you know the risks from the issues is articulating the risk statement. They should be written in "IF" and "THEN" statements.

For example:

_IF_ *our team's primary supplier experiences a catastrophic disruption due to a natural disaster in the August through February hurricane season,*

THEN *we will not have enough supply to support our customers a month after the last shipment.*

Notice I included a timeframe. You want to have that frame of reference of when is your "Vul time" (Vulnerability time).

Remember to include the LIKELIHOOD of this occurring and the IMPACT of it. You can use a scale of 1% to 100% or a smaller scale like 1 – 5 for each of the two.

As for the actions you will take to mitigate, transfer, or avoid, you need to identify when is your "Bingo" (Your point of no return); when will it be too late to do anything? Post that date somewhere. That way you can ensure the right actions are taking place before your team is charting through your vulnerability time window.

There are charts online you can use as templates to make this visual.

82. "Make prudent estimates for when you will deliver."

I've seen many leaders promise a lot and they just can't deliver. An old boss of mine would say, "they got a battleship mouth and a row boat's butt to back it up."

Be prudent in your estimate when you tell your boss or your customer that you will deliver something for a certain date. Give yourself a safety buffer. Don't go too crazy on giving yourself less time but don't make others expect too much of a wait time. Be prudent.

83. "Try to make your decisions as objective as possible."

Making decisions sometimes becomes a foggy situation. There are times that you don't have all the intel. There are other times that you have all the intel, but you have not determined the value of each of your options. I use a Decision Matrix and apply some basic math to it. A decision matrix also helps you reach consensus because everyone sees the math (thought process).

For example, let's say you just moved to another town with your spouse, and you need to both decide where to live and there are two houses you can't make a decision on.

<u>List the things you value in the house</u> (e.g., how close it is to the mall/work/school, how much it costs, aesthetics, etc.).

<u>Assign a weight to each of the values</u> to show how important is each one. They can all be equally important to you, or some can be more important than others. Show it in numbers. You can use percentages or numbers (e.g., 1-5, 1-100, etc.).

<u>Then you rate each house in each of the values you listed</u>. In the scale you use, how much does your House #1 or House #2 meet each of the values? That is your rating.

<u>Then you multiply your weights with their respective ratings under each house</u>.

<u>Finally, you add up the sums of all the products</u>. The one with the higher number is the house you should decide on.

One important thing to consider is that, as you do this, it will reveal much of your thought process. Once your thought process becomes clearer to you, there will be times that you will want to reassess how much weight you assign to a value or how much you rate an option for any given value.

Here is a visual of the example. The intent is to show your team what is important and your collective thought process as you decide and in the end, you will be able to "quantify" why you are going with option #1 or #2.

Values	House #1			House #2	
	Weight*	Rating**	Weight x Rating	Rating**	Weight x Rating
Proximity to work	3	1	3	1	3
Proximity to store	3	1	3	2	6
Proximity to school	2	3	6	3	6
Rent	1	1	1	1	1
Aesthetics	1	1	1	1	1
			14		17

*Weight: How important is each value?

**Rating: How well does this option meet each of your values?

84. "The first casualty of combat will be the plan."

In Afghanistan, a leader I greatly respected shared that once the chaos of combat starts, your plan is usually the first thing to go out the window. But it is essential to plan. It will help you understand everything you can do in response to what can happen in your battlespace. You need to own it.

In life, remember this. Sometimes you get kicked in the teeth and your plan does not come through. You need to understand that it is part of life, and you need to find a positive and successful way to respond.

85. "Garbage in. Garbage out."

Whatever you watch, read, speak, and listen to will feed your thoughts. If you put garbage in, you won't like what comes out. Be intentional about what goes in.

When it comes to management tools like Jira, Sharepoint, or any other tool, keep that in mind; garbage in, garbage out. Those tools won't help you if you're not using them appropriately with the right information.

86. "The meeting before the meeting."

I hate meetings, but there are meetings that you should plan for. If these are external meetings, you should huddle with your team beforehand. I hate to say it, but you sometimes (not in all cases) do need to have a meeting before the meeting.

Ask each other, "How do we want our world to look like after the meeting? How will we shape the conversations? What are the points that we need to share in order to make that happen?" Go into those meetings ready to guide it and shape it in a way that supports your team.

You also want to use that time to identify what your known unknowns are. Perhaps your team can educate them on it. I share a quote with my team, "If I'm walking into a crap storm, I need to know which way the wind is blowing." You need to know the environment you're stepping into when you get to that next meeting.

87. "Empower your team to hit the piñata."

As a Hispanic, I've been to my share of parties with piñatas. The person who is trying to hit the piñata is blindfolded so everyone else is trying to yell which way they should swing the broomstick or bat to hit the piñata. What if the person did not have a blindfold on? No one would need to be yelling which direction they need to swing. You would just need to tell them to hit the piñata. They can make the decisions of how to swing on their own and hit the piñata.

There are leaders who love to keep their team with blindfolds on so they can continue yelling orders and directing them in everything they do. They want to tell you how to swing and direct every motion you do. Leaders should take their team's blindfolds off; help your team see what you see.

Also, never get tired of sharing your vision with your troops. The more they are able to see it, the easier it will be for them to recognize opportunities and make decisions to achieve the vision, even when you are not there.

Create a world at work where your troops have a full visibility of your battlespace where you're operating in and your resources. Once you share with them your vision and intent, they can go and synthesize what is going on to make decisions and execute the mission.

88. "If you're not seeing data, you're not managing. If you're seeing the wrong data, you're still not managing."

This is one of the lessons I learned from a Defense Acquisition University professor. If you want to manage anything, you need to see information that is actionable and can help you make decisions. With the information that you are offered, ask yourself what decisions you can make with those decisions?

If you have the wrong data, it is like being in Cincinnati and trying to get to a location in that city while using a map of San Francisco to get there. You may not make it.

89. "The owner's eye fattens the cattle."

This saying emphasizes the idea that when the owner is present and actively overseeing the care and well-being of their livestock, the animals tend to thrive. It's hands-on management and direct involvement. It is not about micromanaging. It is about being engaged to address the needs of your team. You cannot manage and supervise while being distant.

I've heard young professionals say that they wish they had the top job so they can take it easy. That is not quite how that works. The top leadership jobs keep you busy because to make your team successful, you need to stay engaged, have eyes on.

90. "After advancing in rank, at some point, be ready to switch from team captain to coach."

If you have ambitions to advance in rank, there comes a time where you must flip a switch on your involvement and activity where it will no longer be with the team. Your time as the team captain is done. You are now on the sideline as a coach. If you get into the field, you will lessen the impact your team will have. You must help them be successful while looking at the whole landscape.

This is perhaps the most difficult change leaders go through in their professional growth. Some never make the switch and cannot handle the workload at a senior level because they still want to be involved in everything on the field at the tactical level.

You need to be able to delegate. If you can't, you need to have those serious conversations with your subordinates about why you cannot trust them and what you need from them. If you want to let go and delegate gradually, use the three elements I've mentioned before: Tools, Rules, and Battle Rhythm.

a) Tools: Tell your team what tools you need them to use to report their status on. It can be ppt, word, Confluence, Sharepoint, Jira, etc.

b) Rules: Give them the Rules of Engagement...show them where the boundaries are and what responses they need to conduct in certain circumstances. For example, "If there is an expense over X amount of dollars, report to me."

c) Battle Rhythm: Provide guidance of how frequently you want to be given updates.

In the military, this transition from team captain to coach must happen when the individual goes from the rank of Captain (O-3) to the rank of Major (O-4). Depending on the responsibility given to an officer, it could happen sooner, but that is generally the first big transition. Be ready! As you advance in rank, you will need to delegate while focusing more on strategic issues, resourcing the team, identifying inter-agency solutions, preparing your team for the next 3-5 years (perhaps even 5-10 years), etc.

Delegating can be difficult for some, but you can't run a unit by just telling everyone what to do. You need to equip and empower your team to make decisions on their own. In his book "Without Hesitation, General Hugh Shelton says, "But when a man's ego says 'I don't need anyone's help', that's a pretty good time to start looking for a new leader."

91. "No one likes to be 'red' in public."

For people to execute tasks, you need three things; a task, a due date, and someone tagged to be responsible for its completion. You will have people who test you and ignore your tasks. Make all your given tasks public. Post this on your weekly staff meeting charts.

If they bust the suspense date, then they go "red" and make sure it is colored "red." As you go through the chart in your meeting, if you see red, ask about it. Provide feedback (e.g., "This is unsatisfactory", "This is unacceptable", "Can someone else help?", etc.)

No one likes to show up "red" in public. I wish someone had taught me this when I was a young officer dealing with a team member who never did any work. Once you create a way for these employees to show up "red" in public, they will likely start working to knock out their tasks or looking for another place to work at. Either way, you will win. In the government, this helps you document people's effectiveness in firing those who are not working. If you need to fire them, then this helps you start to build a weekly record of them not being able to complete their tasks. Additionally, it will be in a forum where several people will witness it.

As I've mentioned before, it is common in government organizations that there is one or several people who never do their job but won't get fired. As a leader in the government, I sometimes moved great people to another organization because I knew that is where they would be happier. One time I gave up one of the strongest program managers I had on my team. He was not happy where he was at. He wanted a job with greater responsibility. I gave him to one of my fellow section chiefs because I knew their workload was growing and that would offer our guy a greater opportunity. After a couple months, my buddy told me how big of an impact the program manager had.

However, with people who just don't work, I couldn't give someone else my problems. Sometimes, other leaders have been willing to take them, and we make a switch where we both know what we are getting. I've checked in on them later to see how things have turned out and the person they had transferred from my team had not changed. Their new boss is dealing with it.

The problem in government is that these people have been allowed to stay for many years and they are utterly dysfunctional. Nobody had the backbone to fire them early on. Nothing will wake them from their dysfunctionality. They have the opposite of the Midas Touch; everything they touch turns to poop. When I've had to employ them, I use my table shown below. I make it public, so everyone sees their weekly excuses and their "Red" status. It has not taken long before the ones who are dysfunctional and have failed at completing their work for many weeks have started to look for jobs somewhere else. Not too many people like to stand out negatively, like a turd on a cake. They prefer to leave. Some will "retire" and go work somewhere else. It frees up a billet for you to hire someone who is effective. It works out great if you're able to promote someone else into the billet they leave behind.

Anyways, you can use the table below to show the weekly status. Something to include is guidance for your teammates to write a one-liner or two in the task's status if it is yellow (at risk of being delayed) or red (delayed), explaining what they are doing to get back to green (on time) or to complete it. If the status is green, they can leave it blank or they can provide a short line for their status if that is what you prefer. If a task goes red, keep it red. At some point, you and your teammate can discuss if you should keep it red or re-baseline the timeline. There are cases when you may want to re-baseline, where it makes sense and with people who are fully engaged in executing the mission. Otherwise, I would not even entertain the thought.

You can use this table as a template.

Task	Lead	Start Date	Due Date	Status	Comments/Status
Complete AARs	John	3-Nov	20-Jan	Yellow	Scheduling time to focus on AARs for a week in order to catch up.
Finalize Risk Management Plan	Sarah	22-Sep	13-Oct	Red	Requesting leads to populate risk chart by 9-October. Reviewing risk chart on 10-October
Finalize Budget for 2024	Jen	1-Sep	31-Oct	Green	

Whenever I reviewed this table on my staff meeting slides, I tried to have a funny meme or video in the previous slide. That way we could laugh and have some fun, before going into serious conversations regarding our high priority taskers and their Green, Yellow, Red statuses. I learned this tactic from an old boss I worked for during my staff tour.

92. "Have an artifact."

In recent years, many have done away with PowerPoint or other types of documentation. They prefer to just talk, and they say that if you talk regularly, it helps everyone stay on track until the project is executed. Not true. Have a visual! These regular conversations become what an old sergeant used to call a "BOGSAT", Boys and Girls Sitting Around a Table. A BOGSAT meeting did not conclude with a plan and there is no visual of your timeline or battlespace. A team needs an artifact they can look at and know what is next. If you don't like PowerPoint, that is fine. Use something else but have a visual your team can look at. Your team needs to be able to look at their battlespace in several dimensions; space, time, teams, actions, priorities, etc.

Never underestimate a visual. Two of my experiences showed me how much a visual can facilitate your efforts to grow a team and build consensus on tough decisions.In my first experience, I saw one of my project managers and one of my engineers discussing their plan on delivering some cabling to a facility we needed to equip with new technology and how we were going to establish connectivity of different capabilities. I listened to them, and they were both saying different things, but thinking that the other one was agreeing with everything they said. I let them go for a solid 20 minutes, at least.

Once they were getting ready to break, I asked if they were ok. They said they were. Then I asked one of them, "Please draw on the white board what it is that your plan looks like and your timing." This is often called a Rehearsal of Concepts (ROC) Drill. It is pronounced "Rock" Drill. The engineer started drawing his timeline and the important checkpoints that he was tracking. For example, he depicted the meeting times and locations with the contractor who was supporting the team, the actions he was taking to mitigate risks, the support times for when our Logistics Team was going to engage, and the key delivery milestones with their respective location. As he was drawing on the white board, the project manager who had agreed with him this whole time jumped and said, "That was not what I was saying at all. I can't support that!"

On another occasion, my chief engineer was talking to one of our stakeholder representatives. Both were arguing, but they were actually saying the same thing. This is what is called a "Violent Agreement". They were in, no-kidding, a "Violent Agreement". As I saw each of them get a little bit frustrated trying to explain their position, I asked one of them to draw their plan on the white board. Just a few seconds went by when the other one shouted, "That is the same thing I'm saying!"

Never underestimate the power of conveying a message with a visual. I asked each of my project managers for a "slide deck" briefing with the following slides to make sure we had a visual and we were all on the same page.

Slide 1: A narrative of the original requirement.

Slide 2: A visual of the requirement.

Slide 3: A visual of the solution.

Slide 4: The timeline showing how long it would take to deliver and key milestones.

Slide 5: The chart with the requirements and money they needed, and the dates for when

the money had to be in place.

Slide 6: All contracting details

Slide 7: Risks

Slide 8: Challenges they needed my help on or our senior leadership's help.

The project managers fought me on this because they didn't see a point to it. That briefing each one put together was our artifact we could use to reference how each line of effort was doing. Nonetheless, one of them came back to tell me that one of our stakeholders absolutely loved it because it gave them the visibility and context for everything. He apologized for pushing back on this and giving me a bit of a hard time.

Use the back of the napkin if you need to, tailor something to what you need, but never forget to use a visual and an artifact to help your cause. It also creates one "radar" picture view for each person on the team. They all see the same thing on the "radar".

93. "Don't send more than two emails on the same argument."

Keeping in mind that your emails must stay concise, when you send a message and your counterpart replies with a message you want to reply to, let that be your last message via email. If your counterpart replies after that, pick up the phone and talk through the issue or go meet in person. Do not continue to argue via email.

94. "I've rarely seen an organization with high standards and low morale."

A friend of mine heard this from a General officer. People take pride in doing a job well. It improves morale. If you raise the bar with how the team does the job while they are in a slump, it will help the team's morale. You need to do this very tactfully.

95. "Learn the rules before you break them."

Rules are set in place to prevent certain issues. There will be times when your team will face circumstances that no one had ever conceived, even the people who wrote the rule book. Trying to solve the issue, you may trip over the rule book. Don't!

If you know the rules and understand them, you can work through a problem while applying the rules.

Sometimes you may need to throw them away while ensuring you prevent the issues they were there to prevent and still deliver a solution to your team.

96. "<u>If a team is working such a high priority for the boss, the boss needs to keep it safe from the other lunatics running the asylum</u>."

If the boss does not protect the team and gives it the resources (Personnel and Money) they need, other leaders from other teams will try to drive decisions that impact that team's personnel and money. Everyone wants a piece of the pie, especially if it gets their name out there.

This lesson is something I took away from a video where Ajay Banga, then CEO of MasterCard, shared his experience as a leader. He talked about how he saw it as a priority to have new initiatives and understood that it would require serious research. He created a team that would focus on coming up with new initiatives. It was his type of R&D team. He shared that no one could touch it because it was a budget he controlled and allocated to the team.

It is true, big programs attract the attention of many. Other leaders in the organization start wanting to have a piece of it or a say in how it is managed. You need to protect your highest priorities and entrust these to be managed by someone with a safe hand.

97. "<u>Learn from other industries</u>."

Although not everything will translate and apply directly to your industry, there are some great practices and tools from other industries that can be used in yours.

I learned a few great lessons from listening to leaders like Alan Mullaly, Ajay Banga, Jeff Immelt, Jack Welch, Patrick Lencioni, John C. Maxwell, and many other leaders in the private sector. Alan Mullaly saved Ford.

The story of how he did it is captured in the book "American Icon." It was an awesome read! If you watch some videos where he is sharing his principles in leadership, he talks about relentlessly implementing a few I'll list here.

a) People first... Love them up

b) Everyone is included

c) Compelling vision, comprehensive strategy, and relentless implementation

d) Clear performance goals

e) One Plan

f) Fact and data

g) Everyone knows the plan, the status, and the areas that will require their particular attention

h) Respect, listen, help each other, and appreciate each other

i) Emotional resilience—trust the process

j) Have fun—enjoy the journey and each other

It offers a phenomenal framework to employ wherever you work. Alan Mullaly also shares a chart that reflects Green, Yellow, and Red status. It is another tool and lesson that you can apply to any undertaking across multiple industries. I've used it. He shares how the team forecasted a $17-billion loss for that year, but everything at the leadership meeting was colored green. Somebody was not telling the truth. Mullaly says that after that, leaders started to post some things with red. The impact of this was that someone from another side of the room said, "I can help you out with that." Transparency gave way to collaboration.

I can't tell you how I wish this was a common practice in government. In my experience, we were encouraged to not show "Red". Someone has to put a "spin" on it. Middle managers flip out if anyone could suggest that things were not going great. It kills any opportunity for leadership to foot stomp the need for mode collaboration.

Always peak over into other industries to see if something applies to your field.

98. "<u>Don't let too many cooks in the kitchen</u>."

As a brand-new second lieutenant (O-1), my boss gave me a non-mission related project. It was to bring a jet from an Air Force base 40 miles away to the museum we had at the installation where we worked. Having to fill my schedule with non-mission related work always frustrated me because it felt like someone telling you, "We don't need your skills for real work". Anyways, I got over it. In the military, as a young officer, you need to show you can make things happen with anything they throw at you. Otherwise, your boss will start ignoring you and it won't help your career.

The task was to get the airplane to the museum in time for us to have a ceremony in front of it to celebrate the Air Force birthday. The boss had several ideas of how to get the airplane from the base to the museum. Some of my coworkers had their ideas. The engineers had their thoughts too. My boss' favorite idea was to get two helicopters to carry it and place it on a pad at the museum. I called several units that had helicopters. They chuckled. Then I reached out to the crash crew on base to ask for help. They liked the challenge.

The first idea we considered was that we could tow the aircraft through some backroads and get it across the highway and on to the Army post where the museum was. The problem is that we needed new tires because we would not be able to move the aircraft with its old tires. It was not our favorite idea, but it was one we wanted to see if it was feasible.

Since my boss had said, "If you need anything, let me know and I'll make some calls to get you the help you need." I went to him and told him that we needed tires. He came back and said, "Can't get you new tires. Go think of something else. If you need anything, let me know so I can make some calls to get you the help you need." The next idea was to truck it. We could place the airplane on a truck and drive through the back roads to get it to the museum. We needed a crane to lift it and place it on the truck bed. I went to my boss and asked if he could talk to the engineers. They had cranes. He got back to me,

"Can't get you a crane. Think of another idea and if you need anything, let me know so I can make a few calls so I can get you the help you need."

The team and I met at their office. This time, there were many more people in the conference room than from our previous conversations. There were a bunch of other senior folks who had been around the Air Force for a while. They were experienced. They wanted to know what the status of the project was, the ideas we had considered, and I can't remember what else. We discussed the issue. Everyone had a comment. It started to get unorganized and loud with everyone trying to voice their ideas. I ended the meeting and asked the crew to meet me at the site where the airplane was at. None of the other senior folks in that meeting seemed to have a solution that was feasible. None of them were actually part of the core team. I wanted to take the team where they could see the problem and think freely without one of their bosses pontificating over their shoulder.

We met at the site. Some of us remained standing. A few sat down on the tarmac under the plane for shade. We started to brainstorm all over again. How could we get the plane on the truck without a crane? One of the youngest guys on the team started to share his idea with one of the other guys. After a minute, it looked like the other guy really liked his idea. We asked them to share. The idea was to put air in the struts of the aircraft. Then, have our logistician drive the truck bed, backing up, through the middle of both landing gears. Once the aircraft was over the truck bed, they would take the air out of the struts, and it would lower the airplane to rest on the truck bed. We discussed it and everyone agreed it was possible. It worked!

The day we were going to do it, one of my fellow lieutenants told me that our boss was going to be at one of the offices on base where we were supposed to drive by on our way out to the back roads, and that he wanted to see us before leaving. Generally, he was a nice guy, but he had not been of any help. I didn't want this effort to get shut down. Anyways, it was an old plane no one wanted. If it broke on our way there, it broke. No one was going to lose a birthday over this. As we drove by the offices where my boss was at, several people started to come out to see this huge jet being trucked off base. It wasn't a crowd yet, but I got nervous that my boss was going to come out to waive us down. I was driving a government vehicle, following the truck with the airplane. I called the guy driving the truck and said, "Floor it." We continued our journey.

Once we got to the museum, we were able to get the engineers from that base to help us with their cranes to get the jet off the truck and in the park in front of the museum with old missiles and other smaller aircraft. If you ever go to White Sands Missile Range and see an F-4 Phantom at the museum's missile park, that's my bird. We celebrated the Air Force Birthday that year and I was so glad to be done with that project. Nonetheless, the lesson stuck; everyone has an idea but having too many cooks in the kitchen is a real problem. Help the team get away from everyone who has an idea but won't be part of the actual execution. Give the team a place to think, close to the problem where they can think clearly. Get rid of those who love to pontificate. Finally, don't be surprised if your youngest folks come up with the best idea. Recognize them.

99. "Learn how to lead and manage change in your organization."

Change is hard because people overestimate the value of what they have and underestimate the value of what they may gain by giving that up." (James Belasco and Ralph Stayer)

Let's talk about change. Everyone hates it. Leading change in your organization is painful. If you are tasked with leading a project that brings about significant change to your organization, you may want to sharpen your skills in negotiations, change management, persuasion, and communication. I'd recommend reading some material on those topics. John P. Kotter is an expert in change management. You can read some of his work online in the Harvard Business Review.

I took an online course on Change Management from the Defense Acquisition University that had material from the Harvard Business School. I was impressed with the worksheets and information they provided. As you read through the material below, you will see that it is so basic. You may even say "This is stupid" but you would be amazed at how many organizational changes and re-organizations I've been through, and there was never a leader who went through these steps to make the transition more digestible for our personnel. I wish someone would have walked through these questions when implementing change in the organizations I've been in. As basic and easy as they are, very few take the time to walk through this. You could gather this information and plug into a presentation you can share with your team.

One of the first challenges the manager will face in leading change is communicating the change. The course listed several steps and questions you had to answer to prepare to communicate the change to your organization. Here they are.

Part 1. Gather Information about the Change Initiative		
What is the change program and what are its goals?		
Why is the change program taking place?		
What is the scope of the change program?		
What hurdles stand in the way of implementing the change program?		
What are the criteria for success, and how will success be measured?		
How will people be rewarded for success?		

Part 2. Identify Key Stakeholders and How/What you will Communicate to Them.		
Stakeholders:	*Communication approach:*	*Information you will share: (Benefits of change program to this stakeholder & Disadvantages of change program to this stakeholder))*

One of the things I found particularly helpful was a Worksheet for Addressing Resistance to Change.

Use this tool to record the reasons why people are resistant to change and determine next steps for addressing this resistance.	
What comments have you heard or behaviors you have seen that indicate people are resistant to the change program?	What do you think the underlying motivations for these reactions are?
I don't think our group should be merged with another group	People prefer the status quo or feel that change will mean personal loss in terms of security, money, status, or friends. Additionally, Team Delta has had some negative experiences with Team Alpha in the past.

Steps for Addressing Resistance	Yes	No
Have you talked on-on-one with the individuals who are resistant to change to better understand their reactions?		
Did you encourage them to express their thoughts and feelings openly?		
Did you explore their concerns by asking clarifying questions?		
Did you listen carefully to their responses and take their comments seriously?		
Have you communicated the benefits of the change in terms of what might be of value to them?		
Have you incorporated their suggestions into the plan to improve it?		
Have you explored ways to engage these individuals in the planning and implementation processes so that they feel more invested in the change program?		
Did you consider the ways in which you may be adding to their feelings of resistance?		
If you answer "No" to any of the questions above, you may want to rethink how you're addressing resistance to the change program.		

Another tool they offered was a table that would help you as the manager to overcome obstacles to change.

It was a worksheet with a table like this one below. I've filled out the white blocks just to offer an example of how you could fill this out.

Obstacle to Team's Progress	Options for Overcoming the Obstacle	Rank the Options (1=Most promising; 5=Least promising)	Allies, Resources, Special Training
Employees' resistance to change, reluctant to adapt to new software	Employee Training	1	Allies: HR, Training Department Resources: Budget for training
Inadequate Support	Establish a support system	2	Allies: Designated support personnel Resources: Support Desk, Ticketing System
Communication gaps	Creating a Communication Plan	3	Allies: Internal Communication specialist Resources: TBD

100. "Do a hotwash after an event or operations."

Whenever you and/or your team have executed an operation or participated in an important event, do a "Hotwash" or an "After Action Report"(AAR) to understand what occurred, the so what, what did the team do well, and what can the team do better next time.

There are AAR templates online. My advice is to do a Hot Wash. For the Air Force, this is a post-mission debriefing. It is a structured and organized conversation held immediately after an operation or any important event. The term "Hot Wash" comes from the concept that the review takes place while the event is still fresh in everyone's minds, or while things are "hot."

Go through the steps.

a) Describe what happened, in sequence. Draw out your timeline on the board.

b) Explain the "So what?"

c) Identify what was done well.

d) Determine what could have been done better.

The biggest pitfall I have seen in Hot Washes for teams is that someone mentions someone else's name in a negative manner.

For example, one of the items a member would like to discuss could be the travel schedule of a trip, "Bob scheduled our travel on a Sunday and didn't even stop to think about our families during that day. He preferred a non-mission essential business trip on a family day rather than allowing us to spend that time with our family. He should have left travel for the work week." Instead, speak to the facts without the names. Here's a better example in the table below.

Time	What happened	So what	Did well	Must do better
T – 6 days	We were scheduled to fly on a Sunday	It took an important time, and we should have spent it with our family instead of a business trip. It contradicts senior leaders' guidance to take care of our families.		Coordinate events so that the team does not need to travel during a day they spend with their families. We've been outspoken about the need for family time. Our planning needs to reflect it.
T - 0 Days	Team members traveled to conference destination via different flights	Some members scheduled a late flight and the flight got delayed into the next day		Schedule every member on the earliest flight for the day.
T+1 Days	Several members did not see the itinerary for the week	Some members were not aware they were supposed to attend a few classes during the week of the trip		Itinerary should be posted in a central location as well as generally distributed to all members who will be participating.
T+2 Days	Senior leaders met with their counterparts while having subordinate leads in the room	We were able to glean how the other team's roadmap looked for the next few months and it helps us posture to take advantage of their new ideas	Senior leaders met with their counterparts. The subordinate team members were included.	

Keep personal names out. Speak to the facts. The feedback we provide here already pokes at someone. If they're part of the conversation, they should help list everything that happens and should be ready to own the part of the operation they could have done better. No need to throw a dart at a name.

Not including names minimizes defensive reactions. When people feel they are getting attacked or blamed for something, they become less inclined to discuss their experiences or insights of what transpired. Keeping the names off also facilitates keeping a positive atmosphere that is blame-free. That encourages collaboration and constructive feedback. This can result in much more problem-solving and a stronger working relationship to work together towards shared goals. <u>Handle cases where there NEEDS to be individual accountability, separately</u>; not in the Hot Wash.

101. "<u>Anyone who tells you that there is one solution that fits all, has no clue of what they are doing</u>."

There is no panacea that fixes everything.

20 to 30 years ago, the methodologies that people would preach as panaceas were TQM, Lean, TOC, and a couple others. In recent years, it has been "Agile." There have been people who will point you to Agile for everything.

Anyone who tells you that there is one solution to everything does not really know what they're doing. These spectacularly incompetent individuals personify the adage, "If all you have is a hammer, everything looks like a nail." They think that the hammer (or whatever tool they've fallen in love with) is the solution to everything.

In recent years, it has been "Agile." As I've seen it applied in the units I've been in, Agile is near-sighted. When everything becomes short-sighted instead of creating a tailored management approach for your team that also includes a strategic perspective, the program will be as agile as a large airline airplane doing a barrel roll. It will be agile, once. One of my peers came to me halfway through the year asking for a large sum of money for a Technical Refresh on our equipment. He had not budgeted for it because Technical Refreshes are planned three years out and the way they implemented Agile was only looking 3 – 6 months ahead.

I'm sure more than at least one Agile practitioner reading this may be saying "It should have been in the backlog and identified as a requirement at the appropriate time." Stop trying to jam everything into Agile. Instead, make Agile align to your organizational needs.

I've run into several leaders telling their organization that one of their strategic objectives is for the organization to "Be Agile." For them, Agile turned into an end and not a means by which we could execute our mission. As I heard everyone talk in the meeting, they were so focused on looking Agile that no one really talked about the capabilities that were supposed to be delivered to our "customer", in our case, the warfighter. I've been in several organizations that claim to be "Agile", and they suffer from the same issues.

The case of Agile is a prime example of how people come to believe that there is one solution that fits everything. Especially those who are not seasoned managers. Some of them may be very senior leaders at the C-suite level. They don't realize that strategic objectives should be more closely related to the core purpose or mission of the organization, rather than being focused on specific methodologies. When setting strategic objectives, it's important to consider the broader goals and outcomes the organization needs to achieve. These objectives should align with the organization's purpose and mission. To use an example from industry, the objectives can be framed around increasing market share, expanding into new markets, improving customer satisfaction, improving product quality, increasing savings, or increasing profitability. Agile can be a factor that enables organizations to achieve those objectives by responding quickly to the environment and/or emerging customer needs. Tools and methodologies are to be considered strategic enablers, not the ultimate objective and certainly not the ingredient that fixes everything.

For the record, I am not against Agile. In fact, I drove our introduction and implementation of Agile in one of my jobs as a captain (O-3) before "Agile" became a buzz word in the Air Force. I'm just against how many people apply Agile. At the end of the day, what you really need is flexibility. Create as much flexibility as you need in your processes, and you don't even need to call it "Agile.

The problem with people who have drunk the whole Agile Kool-Aid and bathed in it is that they don't believe in tailored solutions. They think everything needs to be "Agile." This is the latest example of a panacea people come to believe in as the solution to everything. Regardless, these are some of the issues that the team will likely run into if they see it as a "one-size-fits-all" solution.

a) Lack of Customer Focus: I've seen with my own eyes that organizations prioritize Agile for its own sake rather than using it as a tool to enhance customer centricity and responsiveness. There is an organization I was part of that had a strategic goal of "Be Agile" when that is a means to an end. This objective was set by a C-Suite leader. I've witnessed leaders lose focus. They lead the organization to focus too much on Agile ceremonies and processes, losing sight of the primary goal, which is delivering value to customers.

b) Misalignment: Agile does not automatically align to the organization's truly needed strategic objectives, leading to confusion and a serious misallocation of resources. I've seen where leaders allocate personnel to teams for the purpose of being agile even when that team is not as busy as other teams. I've also seen leaders create matrixed organizations for the purpose of being "agile" and overload all the teams under them because there is someone they can label a lead for every effort. That does not mean they have the right resources to get it done.

c) Checklist Mentality: Teams can treat Agile practices as a checklist to complete rather than embracing the Agile mindset of continuous improvement and adaptation.

I used Agile for this lesson just as an example of how people can hyper focus on one thing and believe it to be the solution to everything. You could come up with a host of other examples.

102. "<u>Know when you need to let things break</u>."

There are times that everyone has "drank the Kool-Aid" and they won't listen to your point of view.

Always speak up well in advance to tell the leadership if something is going to fail or break. If they are

not listening to your point of view, in order to take care of your team, you may need to let things break so the larger team and leadership will realize their mistake and turn around to support your team. There is no greater evidence of a need than when things break. Just make sure you forecast it and mitigate the effects.

103. "Sometimes you need to take the glass half full."

To be an effective manager, you will, from time to time, need to negotiate things for your team.

You're not always going to get everything you ask for. Einstein said that character is what you do with what you have. Take what you have, even if it is a glass half full, and run with it—make the best of it. Don't fall on your sword for something that is not a showstopper for your team. Take it and keep moving forward.

104. "Give the extra money back, early."

You do NOT want to get caught towards the end of the fiscal year of your organization and jumping through flaming hoops to find ways to spend the extra money before the fiscal year ends. Track your money with rigor, closely, every month. Be ready to give any additional funding back to your leadership early enough so everyone has time to assess where it can be used, with a prudent time buffer before the fiscal year ends. Do not wait until a couple months at the end of the year.

Some will tell you that you never give money back and they just try to spend it all. Manage it well and look out for the larger team. If you somehow have extra money, give it back. It could help out your larger organization. If you had extra money because your estimates were poor, find a way to improve your estimates for the following year. Make them solid.

Don't hide poor estimates by trying to burn through the residual funding you may have in your organization's accounts. Your leaders and subordinates will trust you more when you are transparent.

105. "<u>Be ready to explain what will break if the team does not get the funding they requested</u>."

When your team submits the requirements to you for what they need the next fiscal year's budget, ask them to clarify the following:

a) Requirement

b) Describe what they will do with the money they receive

c) Explain what will break if this requirement is not funded

d) Share when this money is needed

Seeing all this information in one visual will help you prioritize your requirements and go down the line to determine where your "waterline" is to mark where funding gets cut off.

All requirements under that could be submitted for "Unfunded Requirement Requests", with your permission. Perhaps they could get funded with any residual funding from the larger organization.

This in turn will help you submit your requirements to your leadership. When you're ready to explain to your leadership what you will be able to do with the money as well as what will break if you don't get that funding, you will be more likely to get the money your team is asking for.

Pay close attention to understand the impact of not getting one of your requirements approved. Explain what will break if that bill is not paid.

There are managers who can write flowery requirements that sound like we're funding something amazing. Ask for the impact of what will happen if the requirement is not funded. You will see if their requirement is something that makes an impact or if it is something as useful as a cup of decaf. If you're presenting your requirements, be ready with a solid explanation of what you need and why you need it, to include what happens if your team does not receive it.

During budget reviews, look out for "Gold Watching" or "Rolexing" from your peers. It's gamesmanship they should not be doing, but it happens. You can catch them in the act if you ask good questions like "What breaks if you don't get that money?" The way they do "Gold Watching" is that they move their low priority requirements up to be their highest ranked budget lines. Since they're so highly ranked, and sometimes labeled "Must Pays", no one questions them. They move their high priority requirements to their lower ranked budget lines, where they will need to defend their requirements and they will have a more compelling explanation. They will easily get approved for their lower ranked priorities since their defense is strong. Then when it comes to their highest ranked requirements, they'll say, "These are my highest requirements and I can't let them not get funded" and no one will say anything so they get everything funded when perhaps the lower priority needs that they moved up should have probably been reviewed, assessed, and cut. It is like if they show those highest priority budget lines and say "Well, this is my Rolex. A super expensive heirloom. It is so valuable; I can't give it up." No one will question it. No one wants to make someone else give up their most valuable thing. If you notice that one of those "Must Pays" is not clear, you can pipe up and ask, "just for my edification to understand our battlespace more, what happens if we don't fund those?"

Be ready to defend your requirements by articulating what breaks if those bills are not paid. Be ready to poke holes at others' potential "Rolexes." Below is the best table I've seen to make everyone's requirements transparent.

Priority	Requirement	Cost	Funded	Description	Impact
1	Analysis suite	$10K	TBD	Buy new database analysis suite	Team will not be able to process data from repair technicians in a timely manner
2	Oil Tube Redesign	$13K	TBD	Re-design tube to add safety feature	Fleet will need to be grounded in a year if design is not fielded by March of the next fiscal year
3					

Something else you want to keep in mind as it relates to requirements, there are senior officers who love to task junior leaders with a new project. If it is not a funded requirement, speak to your senior leaders and verify that they are willing to support the effort, drive resources to you, and fund it. Otherwise, they are just using you for something that is non-mission essential and has no political capital. If it is a requirement without money, it is only a dream, and not a real requirement. Don't get stuck managing a project that doesn't make that big of an impact on the mission to warrant funding.

As for execution, your budget plan is telling leadership, "I'm ready to invest this money for our customer or for our organization." Be ready to invest it or put it on contract as soon as you get it. If you delay, leadership will not trust your timing and budgeting skills the following year. Senior leaders will think, "This money is just standing there. We should have invested it somewhere else because they are not doing anything with it."

Leaders know there is no such thing as a free lunch so if your money is sitting in your account, they will know you're not executing towards your annual objectives. If your execution gets behind 10%, it is going to be difficult to recover. Plan to execute your funds as early as you can in your fiscal year. If you get the money and delay in negotiating your contracts and can't expend your approved budget before the year ends, you will lose that money for the year. Your leaders will see you as someone who lost their opportunity to invest that money somewhere else. If you're in the government, that is money that should be invested in something that improves resources or our national defense for the benefit of the taxpayer.

When your fiscal year starts, take your requirements and put them on a table where you can see when your money will be executed throughout the year. Below is a chart you can use. You can lay out how much you will be executing each month. Meet with your team, including your financial manager, to ensure your execution is going according to plan. If you need to shift, that is fine, but you are aware of your financial execution plan and ready to make informed decisions. In some instances, if you have residual funding in one line of accounting, you can use it to cover additional costs in another effort. It's what we call "doing some internal healing" or "spreading the peanut butter." However, get approval from your leadership if this is allowed. Sometimes it is not.

In the following page, you will find view of a template I use just to track our budget execution. For Profit & Loss management, you'll need a few more rows to cover that data and include it in an image you can look at the whole thing.

Priorities	Requirements	Approved Budget	Jan	Feb	Mar	Apr	May	Jun	Jul	Aug	Sep
1	Personnel	6.000	0.400	0.400	0.400	0.400	0.400	0.400	0.600	0.600	0.600
2	Rent	0.080					0.010	0.010	0.010	0.010	0.010
3	Utilities	0.008					0.001	0.001	0.001	0.001	0.001
4	Technology	0.750			0.060	0.100	0.200			0.390	
5	Marketing	1.000	0.250	0.300	0.450						
6	Supplies	0.020	0.006		0.002			0.010			0.002
7	Depreciation	0.040			0.010			0.010			0.010
8	Insurance	0.020	0.005		0.005			0.005			0.005
	TOTAL	7.918	0.661	0.700	0.927	0.500	0.611	0.436	0.611	1.001	0.628
		Cumulative	0.661	1.361	2.288	2.788	3.399	3.835	4.446	5.447	6.075
		Forecast	0.661	1.361	2.288	2.788	3.399	4.225	4.836	5.447	6.075
		Delta	0.000	0.000	0.000	0.000	0.000	-0.390	-0.390	0.000	0.000
		Forecasted Execution	8%	17%	29%	35%	43%	53%	61%	69%	77%
		Actual Exection	8%	17%	29%	35%	43%	48%	56%	69%	77%
		Delta (Difference)	100%	100%	100%	100%	100%	91%	92%	100%	100%

Execution Percentages	
100%	
90% < 100%	
<90%	

Notes: Decimal in the millions.

Expenditures/Months that have already been executed are colored grey.

106. "<u>Before the next year starts, gather your team and identify your goals/objectives, results, and actions</u>."

Another framework that has been used in recent years is Objectives and Key Results (OKRs). Andy Grove introduced the term OKRs in the seventies. It recently became popular in my circles. Before then, I used "Strategic Goals, Objectives, and Actions". For this case, let's stick to OKRs.

Your Objectives need to be Specific, Measurable, Achievable, Relevant, and Timebound. Review the following for a better understanding.

a) SPECIFIC: Goals should be clear and specific. They need to answer who, what, where, when, and why. Write your goals so they are easy to understand what it is that you are after.

b) MEASURABLE: Goals need to include clear criteria for measuring progress and success. Those can be one or more metrics.

c) ACHIEVABLE: Goals should be realistic and attainable. You should aim as high as possible, but your goals need to be feasible. Don't try to boil the ocean.

d) RELEVANT: Goals should be aligned with your mission and your team.

e) TIME-BOUND: Goals must have a deadline.

f) STUCKEE: I've added this one. Each goal needs a "stuckee", the person stuck with the job of making this happen. An old boss of mine used this term to keep some light humor. That is, a person who will lead the rest of the team in reaching that goal by its due date.

In the OKR framework, Objectives are a little broader that highlights a desired direction. Objectives are more qualitative than goals and more specific. For example, an Objective can be "To become a leader in sustainable technology solutions." For Goals, it could be "To increase our market share by 10% within the next 12 months." Whether you apply Objectives or Goals, just make sure your whole team below and above you, are on the same page.

Your Key Results, in the OKR framework, resemble our definition of Goals above. They are specific, measurable, and time-bound outcomes that indicate the success of an objective. These are what will tell you "We arrived!" Each objective can have multiple Key Results.

Below your Key Results, you will have your Actions or tickets that you will have somewhere like Jira or any workflow management system.

Something that teams regularly miss is assigning a lead for their objective, key result, and tasks. Always have a lead and a due date. You need those two pieces of information to drive execution as well as to help the team prioritize it accordingly.

Here is an example of an Objective, its Key Results, and its Actions (i.e., Tickets) needed.

<u>OBJECTIVE:</u> Increase Customer Satisfaction.

KEY RESULT #1: Achieve a Net Promoter Score (NPS) of 75 or higher by the end of the quarter.

TICKET OF WORK 1: Conduct a customer satisfaction survey to measure the current NPS.

TICKET OF WORK 2: Analyze survey results to identify areas for improvement.

TICKET OF WORK 3: Develop a plan to address the issues identified in the survey.

TICKET OF WORK 4: Implement changes and improvements based on the plan.

TICKET OF WORK 5: Schedule and Conduct a follow-up survey to measure the NPS after the changes.

TICKET OF WORK 6: Analyze the post-improvement NPS and assess progress.

KEY RESULT #2: Reduce average response time to customer inquiries to less than 2 hours by the end of the quarter.

TICKET OF WORK 1: Review the current customer inquiry handling process.

TICKET OF WORK 2: Identify bottlenecks or inefficiencies in the process.

TICKET OF WORK 3: Revise the process to streamline response times.

TICKET OF WORK 4: Train support staff on the new process.

TICKET OF WORK 5: Monitor and track response times daily.

TICKET OF WORK 6: Make necessary adjustments in real-time to meet the goal.

Note: Your OKRs could give you great material to include in next year's performance report/appraisal. You just need to lead your team in execution and achieving your OKRs.

107. "Make actions, results, and impact stand out in your subordinates' performance reports (i.e., personnel appraisals), and yours!"

When you're writing your subordinates' appraisals, think of what they did (Action), Who they impacted (Qualify), and how much of an impact (Quantify) are they delivering.

When it comes to Qualifying what they've done and writing down who your subordinate impacted, think of proper nouns and titles vs nouns. It is better to say they impacted the "ABC Company Research & Development Division" than the "research team." It is better to say that they met the vision of the "CEO" than the "highest ranking executive." These are basic examples.

When you try to Quantify the impact of your subordinates, consider how much money they saved, the time they saved, the number of people they supported, etc.

As you write your subordinate's appraisal, make sure it is clear what action they did. Avoid phrases like "Worked on." Write clear actions; orchestrated, guided, directed, crafted, wrote, led, facilitated, grew, established, etc.

See the following as examples. I've written in blue font the sections that stand out for their qualifying and quantifying nature. The action word is in bold black font.

a) Emily **guided** ABC's 2023 Market Expansion Strategy; enabled operations to start in South America, Europe, and Africa markets, resulting in a 30% increase in international sales and a revenue growth of $2M.

b) Vernon **streamlined** ABC's Production Division's manufacturing process, reducing production time by 20%, which led to a cost reduction of $250,000 per quarter.

c) Jane successfully **managed** the R&D Software Increment 5.0, delivering it three weeks ahead of schedule, which allowed our ABC Sales Division to launch the solution in time for the Cyber Veterans Association event.

d) Bill **created** a new Rehabilitation Department Support Request system, enabling expedient requests to be delivered to the ABC Hospital Chaplaincy Office, ensuring timely pastoral care was given to 57 patients and resulting in reducing cases of patient anxiety by 73%.

Some organizations teach that you should write these achievements using the STAR method; Situation, Task, Action, Result. Others say to use the AIR method; Action, Impact, Result. Whatever you need to use, make sure you highlight the Action and the Impact. You need the What and the so what. Writing your employee's appraisal and just saying how great they are to work with is a disservice to them and it would be evidence that you're not really managing.

108. "You can't care more about a project than what your leadership does."

There are project managers who will tirelessly advocate for their projects even though getting support is like pulling teeth. They grow frustrated, burned out, cynical, and negative because some other project took their people and their money.

It is great that leaders care so passionately about a project, but you need to keep in mind the bigger picture. The highest priority is to keep your larger organization well. You can't use horse blinders and ignore the rest of your organization. In other words, you can't spend all your resources on one toy if your family is going to be left without groceries for the next year. You need to take your project hat off and put your family hat on to think in more strategic terms.

If your project does not have as strong support from senior leadership as you'd like, here are things you can do to advocate for your support.

a) Make sure the project aligns to the larger organization's priorities

b) Communicate the value and potential impact of your project

c) Measure the impact and outcomes of the successes of your project as well as the outcomes if it is not provided the right support by a given date

d) Stay adaptable to support emerging needs in the organization

In some cases, it won't matter how much you convey the impact of not supporting the program, senior leadership will not support it and can even shut it down. In those instances, think outside the box. If nothing works and you believe strongly about that project, it may be time to consider going to another organization and pursue opportunities there that align with your passion.

Just remember to not sacrifice your family life or your mental, emotional, and physical health for a project.

109. "Don't break unity of command."

A greater portion of my career has been in the Acquisition field, where we develop, deliver, sustain, and retire technology. We have mirrored some organizational frameworks found in the private sector. Some of these attempts to use private industry's best practices have broken our Unity of Command in several teams I've worked with.

Matrixed Organizations

The first one I'll mention is the matrixed organizations. We've often used the matrixed organization for when we have limited personnel and we assign them to support multiple project leads while reporting to a functional lead above them. This is where each employee supporting your project reports to two bosses, the project lead, who is the informal boss, and the functional manager, their actual supervisor. On the next page you will see an example of a matrixed organization.

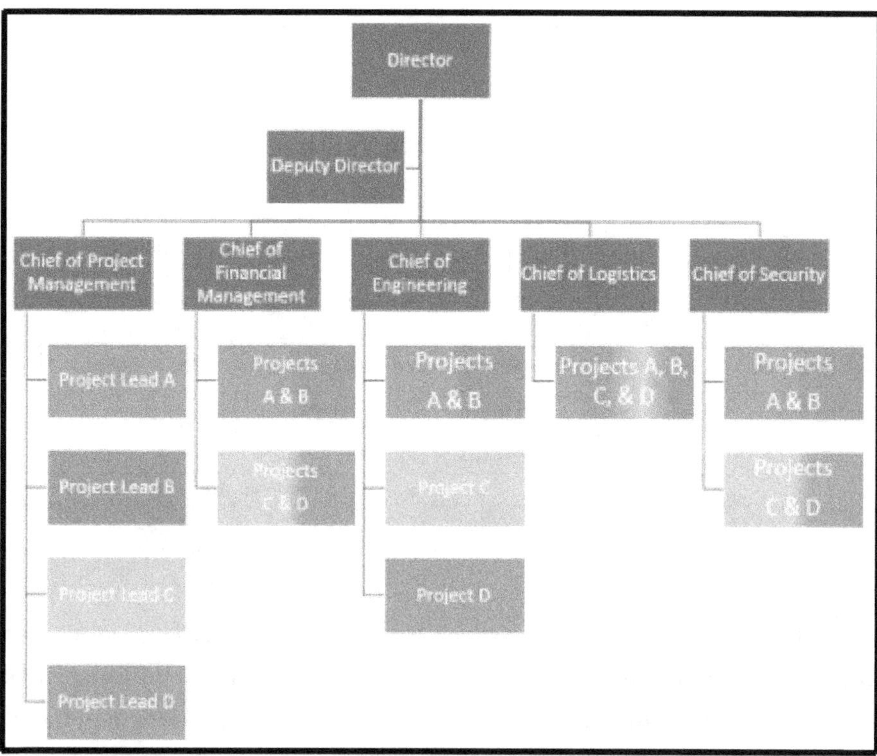

With employees who have two bosses, I've seen Unity of Command broken in several teams because each one has different priorities. Additionally, each employee typically manages multiple projects, so this construct also limits the time that the employee has to concentrate on each effort. In the government, working in a matrixed organization has been a painful experience for me. You're constantly trying to fight for timely support. By the time you move on to your next assignment, you may leave with an ulcer.

What drives further division and limits the ability to create Unity of Command is that each member of a matrixed team has their own equities. Each member has one formal boss and an informal team lead. We've witnessed this. With very few exceptions, the members on the team have different equities. While I've worked with some incredible professionals in a matrixed organization, it has made it painful for us to deal with the rotten apple or lazy teammate because we don't have any authority over the individual. The matrixed org chart makes it easier for poor performers and their managers to have their way with their own priorities. The table below shows an example of worst-case scenarios of each teammate having different priorities.

Team Member	Priority
Program manager	Deliver quality solutions to the customer in a timely manner
Contracting officer	Does not want to go to jail
Security	Says "No" to everything because they also don't want to go to jail
Finance	Produce financial documents they can understand but not anyone else on the team
Engineer	Work through mountains of paperwork and process for additional technical reviews
Logistician	Work through every checklist and process there is

Another worst-case scenario is if the Program Manager gets stuck on stakeholder alignment with an extreme focus on consensus building, risk avoidance, resource optimization, and/or other areas of program management.

The top priority for all of us is to deliver quality solutions to the customer in a timely manner. Everyone should have that priority as their #1. If we do #1 the right way as a team, the other issues take care of themselves.

Unfortunately, out of six matrixed teams I've worked with, only one got it right and everyone worked together as a team. The other ones had people focused on their priorities and even their own timelines, which were different from the team lead's!

For matrixed organizations to work, the organization must ensure the following:

a) The senior leader must clarify what the priorities are (This helps each member temper or focus their attention and manage their project schedule accordingly).

b) There should be enough people to support all the projects and not overload one person in a section where they are supporting multiple projects.

c) Everybody's project clock starts and ends at the same time. There should be one timeline for each project and transparency in how each member is supporting each step of the plan, whether they are on time, delayed, or at risk of being delayed.

d) The senior leader must delegate the proper level of authority to the right people.

You'll notice a couple patterns in this book; one of them is that I recommend transparency as an ingredient to help solve many accountability issues. It is not the only ingredient necessary, but building transparency into your work is a solid step. Transparency that makes an individual's work and impact visible to their peers and senior leaders has a way to pose the threat of professional public humiliation, and it spurs most people into action.

<u>Agile Methodologies</u>

The other thing we've mirrored private industry within recent years is Agile methodologies. These methodologies can be effective but they've negatively impacted some of the teams I've worked with because the senior leaders use the Product Manager position with ill-defined roles, so they end up conflicting with other leadership roles on the team like the lead engineer and project manager.

I was constantly fighting with my leadership in an assignment I had where a Product Manager was telling the team to do one thing and I was telling them to do something else. It was an infuriating situation that went on for almost three years, and it wasted so much time.

If you explore the internet, there isn't an agreement anywhere of what each role entails within Agile, Product Manager vs Product Owner. Tailor your solution to your team and define the roles for each member. Let everyone know what each member's role is and what authority levels each one will have.

Patrick Lencioni says, "Politics are unresolved issues of senior leaders." Don't ignore the issues, create transparency, provide clarity in your direction and priorities, define each member's roles, and empower the leaders serving under you. Otherwise, you will break the Unity of Command in your organization and there will be too much conflict and uncertainty.

NAVIGATING YOUR CAREER PATH

110. "<u>Be part of the main mission</u>."

A great leader I served with shared that when he started out his career, he was in the IT department for a big company that sold consumer goods, mostly personal and household care products. He shared with his boss that he had dreams of climbing the ladder and being part of the senior executive leadership of the company. His boss told him, "You're in the IT department of a company that makes and sells soap. If you want to grow in this company, you need to be really good at making and selling soap." He then applied for a job in an organization that was more aligned with the field he had gone to school for. Nowadays, he is a senior leader in the organization where he moved to.

If you want to grow in a specific company, you want to be part of the main mission. There can be some exceptions, but you don't want to be a mechanic at an accounting firm or a lifeguard at a ski resort. The farther you are removed from the main mission of the organization, the less likely you will be to be part of the group of leaders who move up in ranks. Try to be part of the main production, development, or sales of an organization. Be part of the lifeblood.

111. "<u>Far and away the best prize that life has to offer is the chance to work hard at work worth doing</u>." (Theodore Roosevelt)

Pick a job and a field you really like. If you need help deciding, think of the classes you enjoyed in

school, the movies and shows that you enjoyed watching. Think of who you are most "jealous" of? Talk to friends who can help you get some clarity to make a decision.

What someone advised me to do is to make a list of fields you would like to get into. Then ask someone in each field to have lunch with you. Tell them you will pay for an hour of their time and pay for their lunch. When you get to meet them, be ready with a list of questions about their career life. For example:

a) What do you like most about your career?

b) What do you like least about your career?

c) What opportunities are there in your field for someone with your degree?

d) What does a regular day look like?

Along the way, whatever path you choose, remember that "Whatever good things we build end up building us." (Jim Rohn)

112. "If we looked at your career from outer space, it should not look like multiple small bonfires all over the place. It should look like one giant bonfire."

When I first heard this quote, it really frustrated me because I had gotten way different advice as I came up the ranks, and the advice I got made life more difficult for me.

What the quote means is that as you start your career, pick a field you want to be in. Pick a professional community. Stick with it. Continue to grow, there, building up your bonfire. Don't bounce around into different fields.

In my case, I bounced around and ended up being a jack of several trades, and master of none. What is worse, I didn't have a tribe.

I started out doing Test & Evaluation for Airborne Platforms which fell under the Acquisition community but more on the engineering side than the program management side. As a prior-enlisted officer, I hated the Acquisitions field, so I jumped to another field, and then got involved with Space Operations. After a tour, my functional manager pulled me back to Acquisitions to manage Engine programs (Nothing related to my operational exchange tour). Then I got into managing Cyber development within the Acquisitions field.

After having some operational experience, including a tour in Afghanistan, I felt much more equipped to contribute to the Acquisitions field. Regardless, when I came back, no one knew me, and I had to play a little catch up. My records each year reflected that I was usually #1 or #2 among my immediate peers but I didn't have a tribe and you need a tribe that will take care of you.

When you get to your first assignment, get super smart in your tradecraft, but also take time to let your tribe get to know you. Volunteer in events happening around the organization. Get your name out there. While you become an awesome expert and grow in your tradecraft, get your brand known in your tribe.

113. "Rank, titles, and degrees don't say anything about who you are."

Remember that promotion boards are a group of very few people, looking at a piece of paper that barely reflects a portion of what you've done and potentially reflects an exaggeration of what others have done. I've seen what others write in their records. Don't place your self-worth on anything from the promotion board.

Rank and Pay Grade don't say anything about who you are. Your family and your closest friends are the ones who can say anything about who you are. What kind of parent are you? Spouse? Child? Leader? etc. If the military did not offer you the rank you wanted, move on, and grow somewhere else. Don't tie your identity to a uniform or a rank.

You know what else doesn't say anything about who you are? Your academic degrees. I've seen officers who graduated from the most prestigious universities at the top of their class who have been amazing leaders but I've also seen quite a few who could not lead flies to crap. Your academic degrees and rank have nothing to do with who you are as a leader, as a person. Leadership is not just a matter of the brain. It is also a matter of the heart.

For military officers, the military can offer you the career path and promotions up to the rank of Lieutenant Colonel (O-5) plus or minus 1. There is a possibility you could advance farther. But there are so many things outside your control, don't let rank tell you who you are or dictate your value.

This lesson comes from a general officer I worked for. Again, there are so many things that are out of your control in your career path; try not to feel bad if you retire with a rank lower than Lieutenant Colonel (O-5) or perhaps because you did not make it beyond Lieutenant Colonel (O-5).

The best officers I served with were a First Lieutenant (O-2) who had been passed over for Captain (O-3), and a Major General (O-8) which is a C-suite level leadership title. A lesson that has stuck is that rank had nothing to do with the kind of leader they were.

114. "<u>Every job will offer you two out of three things</u>."

I could never stand it when one of my peers would ask a senior officer for advice on how to advance their career, only to hear, "Just do your best where you're at. I don't even know how I got here." What a lie. There is a roadmap. You can follow it or create your own. I've heard lieutenants ask about how they can one day become a colonel or a general. I've seen responses like, "The best way is to be the best lieutenant you can be." That is not everything. That is a half-truth. Being the best you can be in the job you're at is the beginning. Once you start advancing in the junior ranks, then you need to pick the right jobs that will get you to where you want to be. For some senior leaders, someone placed them on a primrose path, and they never had to worry about anything because there was always a sponsor there with guard rails, guiding them to the next step they had to take. For regular Joes like you and me, we need to gather some intel and make some decisions on where we want to go with our career and our whole professional life journey. Get smart on what paths and stages your senior leaders had in their careers. Identify the patterns. Then you need to decide which path you want to take. Use the lesson below to help you.

Every job you take as the next step along your career path will offer you two out of three things.

a) Better pay (Or promotability)

b) Location

c) Experience

Pick two out of three. You will probably end up at a crossroad where you will need to decide. Ideally, you should include your family in the decision.

In my career, this made a serious difference. In two assignments I was able to negotiate, I looked at the experience and insight some jobs would give me in learning more about a specific mission, and it overshadowed another path that hinted at promotability.

I was warned that it would affect me later in my career because there were assignments I had to have at specific phases in my career. If I spent another tour learning more, I would not have enough time in the rank I held to get the assignments that were going to be key for future promotions. Once I got to serve an "X" number of years at a certain rank without those assignments under my belt, I was no longer competitive for future promotions. Well, it affected my potential for promotions in the long run. Although I still got promoted farther than I expected, I could see a glass ceiling up ahead. But I made the decision of the path and experiences I wanted.

Choose the path and experiences that you want. Up to a certain point, you can switch and say, "This time I'm going to go for location because it is where my family wants to go." If for some reason you hit a glass ceiling, your identity is not attached to that organization. Go grow somewhere else!

While I respect my career field's senior officers' views on career paths, I disagree. The path they wanted me to quickly follow would have given me enterprise horse blinders in many ways. I sought experiences that I knew would make me a strong leader with better intuition and discernment across a couple fields that were becoming more critical for national defense. If my decisions placed a ceiling over my career growth, I'm still happy with my experience and ready to grow somewhere else where I can continue to advance my career as a leader. Never attach your identity to an organization.

I share this because I want you to be better prepared to outline the path you want for your current career and whole professional life. Know that each job usually offers you two of three things. At some point, there may be no turning back in that organization's professional development path for you, and you need to be ok with the decisions you take. Also, because you should know that if your organization's leaders don't agree with your career path, there is life after your time there. One of my old bosses used to call it LAAF, Life After the Air Force.

Design your career and path forward.

115. "<u>Between 0 and 4 years of beginning your career, get really smart at your job and compete for awards</u>."

This is when you need to gain depth in knowledge of your tradecraft. Seek leadership jobs and compete for awards to get recognition. This will lead to other opportunities that can push you for promotions later down the road.

The reason you should compete for as many awards as possible is because awards are an arena where you compete directly with your peers. Winning an award and having it in your resume and/or your records shows you stood out among your peers. This will reflect well when you are being considered for promotion. I did not realize this when I was a junior officer. It wasn't until I had been an officer for 9 years, someone told me that I had competitive stratifications but no awards. I had spent my years up to then just worrying about helping others get awards. In my mind, leaders would push you towards the right jobs and give you the stratifications you needed to advance your career. In many cases, organizations will not have a stratification for you in your appraisals to say if you are in the top 10%, 15%, or 20% of your peers. For those cases, it is important that you have recognition and awards in your appraisals and/or resume. Awards can help you get that recognition that helps you get the stratifications and the right jobs. Always compete for those awards.

Look for opportunities to show your leadership and management skills; and compete for those awards every quarter, year, or any other type.

116. "<u>Between 5 and 10 years of starting your career, you can branch out within your own field</u>."

This is when you gain breadth in knowledge of your tradecraft. Learn more about the broader field and community that you are part of. Get a leadership job and grow as a leader. Get your master's degree out of the way soon!

117. "<u>At your 7-year mark, decide if you want to stay or go</u>."

If you go before 4 years, and you are in a large organization, you may not experience everything there is for a junior professional in your organization. You may have landed in a poor team or under a poor leader for your first assignment, and you would not experience the true culture of the larger organization and community. By your 7-year mark, you get a better feel for the larger organization. Also, you can observe if your leaders are grooming you for senior leadership or if they are willing to support you in a particular career goal that is not related to getting promoted to senior leadership jobs. At that point, you can assess "if the juice is worth the squeeze" and either stay or go somewhere else to grow. Just be careful because some leaders will promise you things and leave you chasing rainbows. Be sure to know which way your senior leaders are willing to support your career goals. There are ways to observe if they are supporting you or not.

Alan Mullaly says "Don't manage your career. Follow your dream and contribute." The truth is that when you're under good leaders, they will catapult you forward. However, if you're stuck with mediocre leaders, or with leaders who do not like you, it won't matter how hard you work, you will never move your career forward. You will not come close to being on the path toward reaching jobs in senior leadership or any other career goal you may have. When you focus on following your dream and contributing, and you still see that your leaders are not putting you on a path to grow toward the experiences you want, it is time to go grow somewhere else. Pick another boss! Don't stick around chasing rainbows! Your job is to be excellent at what you do, and your leaders' job is to give you those paths where you can grow. If they're not doing it, it may be time to go at your 7-year mark, or sooner.

How to know if they are really putting you on a career path towards your growth or experience goals and that it is worth sticking around? You will notice that they will set you up to be closer to the experiences you are seeking. If you want to grow to hold senior leadership jobs, you will see them pushing you for high-visibility jobs, rating you above your peers in your appraisals, making you competitive for career broadening tours, pushing for you to be selected for education opportunities, etc. You will see evidence of their support. If you don't see it, do not stick around chasing rainbows. It may be time to leave.

Finally, I will add that when you get ready to leave, don't focus on leaving your organization. Focus on where you're going. In other words, when someone asks about what you're up to, don't talk about how you're leaving this organization because it is terrible or whatever negative reason there may be. Focus on your vision of where you want to go.

118. "<u>If you decide to stay, be clear with your leaders on what your career goals are. Tell them you want to grow for the right reasons.</u>"

When I was a Captain (O-3), I had a couple opportunities to really advance my career. However, when asked about my career goals, I expressed that I was focused on the mission and not rank, and it appears that it cost me those opportunities. They didn't want to support someone who didn't have plans to stick around and continue to grow in rank. The truth is that a higher rank will allow you to make a greater impact on people and the mission. I had been taught that when asked, you should never say that you wanted to be a Colonel (O-6) or a General (O-7+)(Senior level ranks) because that would be a good sign that no one should support you in that endeavor.

There can be some wisdom to this. Thomas Jefferson is quoted saying "Whenever a man has cast a longing eye on offices, a rottenness begins in his conduct." Nevertheless, I did want to stick around to continue getting promoted to a higher office, and I wanted to do it for the right reasons—to serve. After missing a couple opportunities, I didn't want to play that game of "what I should say" anymore. I decided to just go gain experience in certain fields and to continue to grow for life after the Air Force. Nonetheless, if you want to stick around and grow in your organization, for the right reasons, express that to your boss. Be genuine. Just be aware that your leaders and the people around you will see if you are doing your current job for the right reasons as well.

119. "After your 10-year mark, go for jobs on staff with senior leaders, seek greater leadership jobs, see if your organization has a program to send you to school."

These opportunities are ways that your organization can whisper to you that they would like for you to stay with the organization and will invest in your growth and future opportunities. In the military, this is where you seek jobs where you work with other military branches in your same field. It is what we call "Joint" jobs. In business, you can start looking at working where you can collaborate with other teams in your company. It helps you understand where your field fits in with the greater scheme of things.

Some organizations, like the military, will send you to school in-residence. That is always a good sign that they're going to keep you in the running for future promotions and leadership jobs. They're investing in you.

As you go over your 10-year mark, remember that what is ahead of you may be less than what is behind you, at your current organization. Choose your path wisely.

Also keep in mind that if you have continued to advance in rank and title, you may be getting extremely close to where you need to flip the switch to go from team captain to team coach. It will require different work from you and a different perspective.

120. "Know what you're going to look like in 20 years."

This is not to say how you will physically look in 20 years, but what will others see when they look at your resume list of skills? What will they take away when they get to see you, talk to you, and get to know you as they work with you?

Look at it from these different angles. When you see the person sitting at the head of the table at those top executive meetings, what traits do they have? What are the traits you will need to get there? What will they look for on the board you meet as you try to get that top job? Here below is what you want to develop so that you are ready to be that person at the head of the table.

<u>Leadership</u>. If you advance in rank, you want to grow your leadership skills.

<u>Strong communication skills</u>. You need to be able to succinctly explain complex issues without losing context. You must grow lawyerly verbal precision. You need to be able to listen as well. There will be a host of groups waiting to hear what you have to say; employees, investors, your board of directors, customers, and maybe even the media.

<u>Problem-Solving abilities</u>. On your way up, you will face challenges that require inter-departmental solutions. That means you'll need to be able to grow your skills in a way that helps you collaborate with other departments, businesses, and agencies to get to the solution that your team needs.

<u>Financial Insight</u>. You will need a strong understanding of financial management, including budgeting, resource allocation, prioritization, and overall analysis. Bottomline, you need to be a good steward with fairness, rigor, and foresight.

<u>Resiliency</u>. You need to be able to bounce back. You will get kicked in the teeth and if there were a superpower, it is perhaps the ability to get back on your feet after getting kicked down.

<u>Adaptability</u>. The global environment of the information age can be volatile. Leaders need to adapt to changes quickly and help their teams navigate through emerging challenges.

<u>Change Management</u>. You will need to know when you need to drive change in the organization so that it is postured for the future.

<u>Expertise</u>. You need to be good at something. It is best to get familiar with a particular industry, so you have a feel for the market trends, new technology, and the competition. You don't want to step into an industry where you have so many unknown unknowns. Some arenas require implicit knowledge you will only gain from having been in the trenches of that industry or a nearby field. That said, never underestimate the impact of some skills that easily transfer from one industry to another. For example, innovation, problem-solving, leadership, technology, communication, organization, and a few others. If you want to jump into another industry, go for it. There are plenty of examples of great leaders who jumped into a completely different field and made history!

<u>Relationships</u>. When your team faces challenges, you need to be able to talk to other leaders in industry to help your team or to collaborate with your team. That will require negotiations. Your relationships will also help stay apprised of what is going on in their corner of the industry.

<u>Strategic Vision, Planning, & Execution</u>. You must be able to create a clear and compelling vision. Along with that vision, you need to be able to lead your team in executing your strategy, your goals, your OKRs, etc. Flexibility is key, but don't zig zag so much that you cannot achieve your vision.

<u>Assertiveness and Humility</u>. "Before the fall comes pride." Practice humility and stay engaged to address any issues assertively and respectfully.

121. "<u>There will be a difficult fork in the road; 'be somebody or do something'</u>."

Colonel John Boyd was a highly influential Air Force officer. He was instrumental in how the F-15 and F-16 were designed. He noticed that in a career, there is at times a fork in the road, and you will need to decide which path to take.

"'Tiger, one day you will come to a fork in the road and you're going to have to make a decision about which direction you want to go'. He raised his hand and pointed. 'If you go that way you can be somebody. You will have to make compromises and you will have to turn your back on your friends. But you will be a member of the club and you will get promoted and you will get good assignments.' Then Boyd raised his other hand and pointed in another direction. 'Or you can go that way and you can do something- something for your country and for your Air Force and for yourself. If you decide you want to do something, you may not get promoted and you may not get the good assignments and you certainly will not be a favorite of your superiors. But you won't have to compromise yourself. You will be true to your friends and to yourself. And your work might make a difference. To be somebody or to do something. In life there is often a roll call. That's when you will have to make a decision. To be or to do? Which way will you go?'" (Colonel John Boyd)

In my path, I chose to "do" (i.e., experience), for a while. If it led me to promotions, that was great. If not, I was going to be happy with the experience I got before starting my life after the Air Force and a new chapter in my professional life.

You will need to decide what path to take.

122. "The most impacting things you do for your organization and for your country may never get recognized."

You may never get the recognition you deserve. Sometimes it is about the leaders of the organization you are assigned to. When you get nothing, you need to remind yourself why you are serving.

"Do good things and everything will work out" doesn't always turn out to be true. What is always true is "Do good things and you'll be able to live with yourself." You need to be able to live with yourself in who you are to those closest to you without the recognition, rank, and titles you wish you had.

123. "Greatness without integrity is not greatness."

This lesson came from a book called "Humility." It was a great read that was frankly very sobering because it shed light on how easily we can be proud and selfish instead of striving for humility. Pride just does not work. Pride is bad for business. It will not help the home team. Pride also lets other vices creep in and shortly you will not have the humility and the integrity needed to be an effective leader.

I've seen officers fluff up their award packages and their personnel records, sounding as if they saved the world or cured cancer. Some people will tell you that everyone does it, so you need to do it. It reminds me of when some athletes were doping.

Whatever you do, don't let anyone take your integrity. When I was a cadet, one experience stands out in showing me how invaluable it is to have your friends trust your word. It happened with a buddy of mine, Raul, who we would call "The General." He asked me if I could support an event that he and his wife were going to. I mentioned that it wasn't really in my plans to go. After he and his wife talked to me about it a little more, they convinced me to go. So, sure, "Yes, I'll go." She asked, "Do you promise?"

Before I could say anything, he interrupted, "If Jose says 'yes', I know he will be there, and I don't need him to promise." Before then, I never realized how much weight your integrity and commitment can have. When I was an adolescent, I would lie so much to get out of "trouble." After reaching my twenties, I resolved to change my life from lying so much. That experience with my friend felt so great because someone understood where I stood with my word. It felt great that my word had so much weight for my friends. Always strive to live with integrity. This is a lifelong pursuit and not a destination.

124. "The most common way people give up their power is by thinking they don't have any." (Alice Walker)

I would have been so much more effective at my job if I had just confronted my bosses more. There were cases in which I should have confronted them to ask for support and sometimes to say "knock it off". I did it a couple times and I should have done it more. I did not confront most of my leaders because I was trying to rise above their disengagement or any trouble I saw with them; and still make a difference for folks at my level. The lesson is that there are moments when you need to confront your leaders, in a respectful and assertive manner, to get the support you need and the recognition that can support your career, either from them or their boss.

In my career, my first supervisor was racist. He was constantly dropping offensive racial words. He treated me less than how he treated the other guy in the office. In 18 years, he never got promoted past junior ranks. That should have been a sign that he probably should not be supervising anyone, but there he was, shaping young minds. He was terribly negative and that influenced your thinking in a way. Having that influence did set me back a little. The quote, "The power of excellence is overwhelming. It is always in demand, and nobody cares about its color" (General Daniel 'Chappie' James) helped me through that time, but I still wish I had said something instead of putting up with it for a couple of years. He never did anything blatant, and he was always fair on paper, but there were things where you could feel a light sting of racism. It was enough to ruin your day. I did my best. During his farewell, he shook my hand and said, "You're a good dude, Castro".

I was fortunate to have other leaders around the unit who helped me grow and advance my career. If they had not been engaged, there was not much hope for me.

A couple jobs later, a new boss told me, "Your last boss tried throwing your career under the bus. I've observed you and really like your decision making. I'm going to make sure your records look better while we're serving together.

At the end of the next assignment, one of our senior leaders told me, while we sat in his office, "I'm so sorry that your supervisor either reached the peak of his God-given skills or just stopped caring. We'll at least give you a good officer performance report for this last year. You will have a few months left here before you go to your next assignment. If you work hard and have enough bullets that fit in another performance report, we will write another one and give you a solid stratification." This came after three years of hitting my head against the wall and zero recognition. I wish I had said something to my peers or other leaders sooner.

I had done so much there in that assignment and overseas during that same tour. As I've mentioned before, it is important for your career development to get awards. Since we often need to submit our own drafted award packages, I drafted mine and submitted it. My boss just ignored it.

In my next job, the deputy branch chief shared, "I don't know what it is, but the boss has it out for you." I did stand up to this one and actually blew up on him. More on this one later. In the job after that, my commander told me, "You need to get out of here because they won't take care of you in this organization. They will only be taking care of officers in specific career fields. You're an outsider.

After that job, I ended up getting hired for a one-year executive officer tour, serving directly under a major general (O-8), who is an incredible leader. That tour was a breath of fresh air. Yet, for a long time, it felt like I didn't belong anywhere. I had to do my best to contribute to the mission and take care of my teammates while not getting much support.

I should have stood up and questioned what was going on. I could have gotten the support that I needed and at times perhaps some recognition I could have used to propel my career forward. In retrospect, I wish I could have confronted some of my leaders and asked why they were not supporting me. All my peers and teammates were. Why were some of these leaders treating me differently? There have been moments that, as I look back, I wonder if there was more racism than what I would like to acknowledge. I don't know that, but I wish I had been bolder with my leaders and their bosses about the lack of support I got in several phases of my career.

"Advocate for yourself. Do not let your inner voice or the voice of others hold you back." NEVER sell yourself short. If you don't want to stand up to your boss, for several reasons, talk to your peers and your network so the message can make it through the grapevine up to senior leadership. Someone other than your boss can peek into what is going on in your corner of the organization. This may be more prudent. If word gets to senior leaders, they can help keep the right people accountable without affecting you.

On one occasion, I blew up and confronted my boss. I alluded to this earlier. I had asked the deputy branch chief, "Is it me or does the boss have it out for me?" He replied, "I don't know why, but he has it out for you." After months of him going after me, I was done. He was a civilian and two pay grades above me, but I was done. After a meeting with my team where my boss jumped in and pulled the proverbial rug from under me, I ended up blowing up, "I'm tired of your f***ing bulls**t! Where the f**k did you learn leadership?" That evening, I got home and made some tea, to relax. I told my ex-wife, "I may have flushed my career down the toilet today." I was drained.

The next day, arriving at my desk, my boss said, "Can I see you in the conference room?" I told him I'd get a witness because I didn't trust his integrity. He said he would get one of the senior officers. I was ok with that. A few minutes later, the three of us were in the conference room. My boss started by saying how unprofessional I had been and how it would no longer be tolerated. I kept my bearing. When it was my turn, I said, "I'm very sorry for disrespecting you. That is not the person I want to be, but I am really tired of you having something against me. I'm not the only one who has seen it. You criticize everyone on the team, especially me, without offering to teach us anything. I've worked to create tools to help everyone do better. With your experience, you could help us instead of pulling the rug from under me and going after me. I don't want to be disrespectful and unkind to you, but I definitely do not want you to continue being unkind to me. I want to be able to do my job, learn how to do it better, and make a difference in the lives of my teammates." To his credit, life at work changed after that. He had my back several times on several issues after that conversation.

I share that story as an example that you need to say something when you feel that you are not getting the support you need to fulfill your mission. You can't burn yourself out in the process.

Do it respectfully and assertively, before you get to the point of blowing up like I did. The other option is to use your network to get it up the grapevine to senior leaders.

Never sell yourself short. Talk to your close friends if you need to so that you get a better situational awareness of what is going on. Then, speak up and stand up for yourself.

EPILOGUE

I remember when my parents first brought me to the United States. I would cry in daycare because I didn't know how to speak any English. I can still remember the loneliness and fear. It never crossed my mind that one day I would be typing 45,000+ words in English to write a short book on my leadership notes from a career in the United States Air Force. You never know how your story will unfold so never stop dreaming and never quit. I've been so blessed.

After enlisting in the Air Force, I was told that I was a US permanent resident but not a US citizen. Growing up, I didn't pay much attention to my immigration status. Yet now it was something that came up, front and center. I submitted my application to become a US citizen. Several people around base and in my unit submitted their applications too. Several months went by. I started noticing that a couple folks who submitted their packages at the same time I did or after me would get their response from immigration saying their application had been approved and they were only waiting to be scheduled for the oath. I was feeling scared because I had not heard back, but I waited a couple more months. I got more nervous when we got a phone call from our squadron leadership saying that we would likely deploy in a month or two. The conflict in the Middle East had escalated. I drove down to the immigration office. After grabbing a number and waiting my turn, I approached the lady at the window and explained my situation. I had waited for a response to my application, but never got anything. I explained, "I'm not trying to be sneaky or take advantage of the system. I just know that in a couple months, I may not be here anymore. It would mean a lot if I could deploy as an American. If you'd like, I can give you the number to call my first sergeant or my commander." I was not part of any secret unit so telling her that much was safe, as far as I knew. And I really meant what I told her. If anything happened to me overseas, It would have meant a lot to be an American because I was serving this great nation as other Americans were, as other Americans I had looked up to had served. The lady asked me to wait as she went to the back to speak to her boss. After a few minutes, she came back. She asked me to follow her. She led me to an office in the back. I walked in and greeted the lady there, which I assumed was her supervisor. We talked and I explained the situation to her again. She handed me a piece of paper and I heard her say that I needed to answer the questions on the paper.

They were questions I remembered from Social Studies classes and books I had read through school. I answered all of them and handed them back. She looked at my answers and told me, "You answered all the questions correctly. Stand up. Raise your right hand and repeat after me..."

I walked out of that office as a US citizen, an American. I was wearing my fatigues. Although no one else was there to celebrate with me, I felt so proud and so blessed. As an immigrant, President Reagan's words about young Americans finding "a city of hope in a land that is free " and that this country is a "shining city on a hill" still resonate with me. Without forgetting the land where I was born, I have loved this country I call "home". We enjoy freedoms like no other country. I'm so inspired every time I read or hear, "We hold these truths to be self-evident, that all men [and women!] are created equal, that they are endowed by their Creator with certain unalienable Rights, that among these are Life, Liberty and the pursuit of Happiness." I've done my best to serve honorably and to help others in their life journey.

I share this because, first, I want to reiterate never stop dreaming and never quit. Second, we do live in a great country. I know there has been a lot of division in recent years, but we are still a great, noble, and kind nation.

I pray we can do more healing than dividing. I also pray that regardless of where you are serving, whether it is in the private or public sector, wherever you are, that you can make a strong and positive impact in the lives of those around you. Your kindness and leadership can change someone's life story.

Remember that leadership is a lifelong journey of learning. It's about brains but it is more about heart. That is the only way you will be able to transform your organization and your community. The Air Force Weapons Officer's creed is "humble, approachable, and credible". As you grow in your tradecraft and as a leader, try to emulate those characteristics.

Practice self-compassion. There will be setbacks. Get back up. If you need help, get help but never give up.

"With malice toward none; with charity for all." (Abraham Lincoln)

APPENDIX 1 – MOVIES

Here are some movies and shows that you can enjoy while learning leadership lessons from their story. I experienced numerous "aha" moments watching these movies and have kept their wisdom in mind.

- Twelve O'clock High

- The Memphis Belle

- Thirteen Days

- We Were Soldiers

- Band of Brothers

- Remember the Titans

- The Gallant Hours

- Ike

- The Caine Mutiny

- Twelve Angry Men

- Invictus

- Apollo 13

- Moneyball

APPENDIX 2 – BOOKS

Here are some books you can read to learn more on leadership and management. I've read many books, but these are the ones that stand out.

- 21 irrefutable Laws of Leadership (John C. Maxwell)

- The SPEED of Trust (Stephen M. R. Covey)

- The Four Obsessions of an Extraordinary Executive (Patrick Lencioni)

- The Five Dysfunctions of a Team (Patrick Lencioni)

- American Icon (Bryce G. Hoffman)

- What it Takes (Stephen Schwarzman)

- George Washington's Leadership Lessons (James C. Rees)

- The Culture Code (Daniel Coyle)

- The 7 Habits of Highly Effective People (Stephen R. Covey)

- Never Split the Difference (Chris Voss)

- Radical Candor (Kim Scott)

- The Bigs (Ben Carpenter)

- Extreme Ownership (Jocko Willink and Leif Babin)

- Measure what Matters (John Doerr)

- A Passion for Leadership (Robert M. Gates)

APPENDIX 3 – AIR FORCE RANKS

Air Force Enlisted Ranks

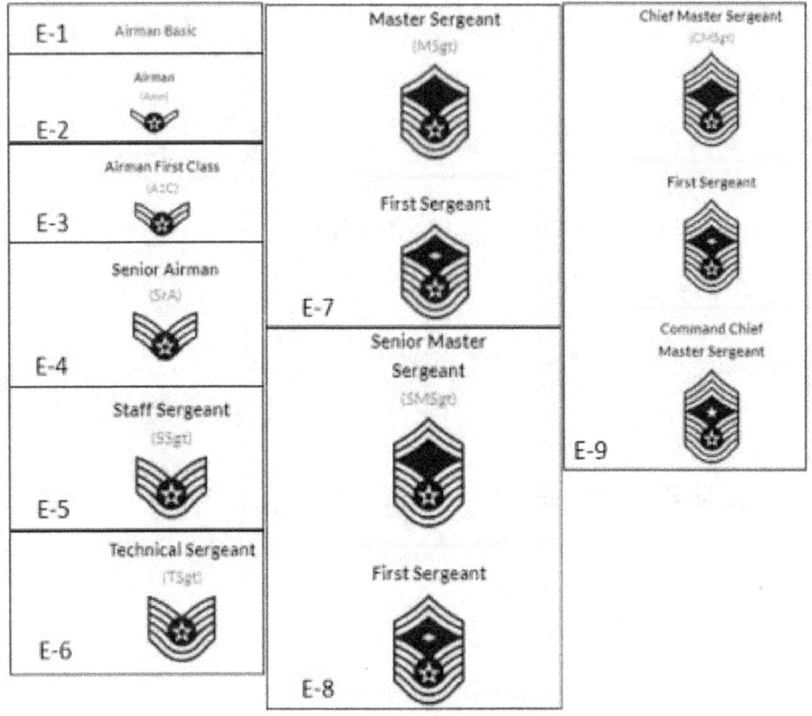

Air Force Officer Ranks

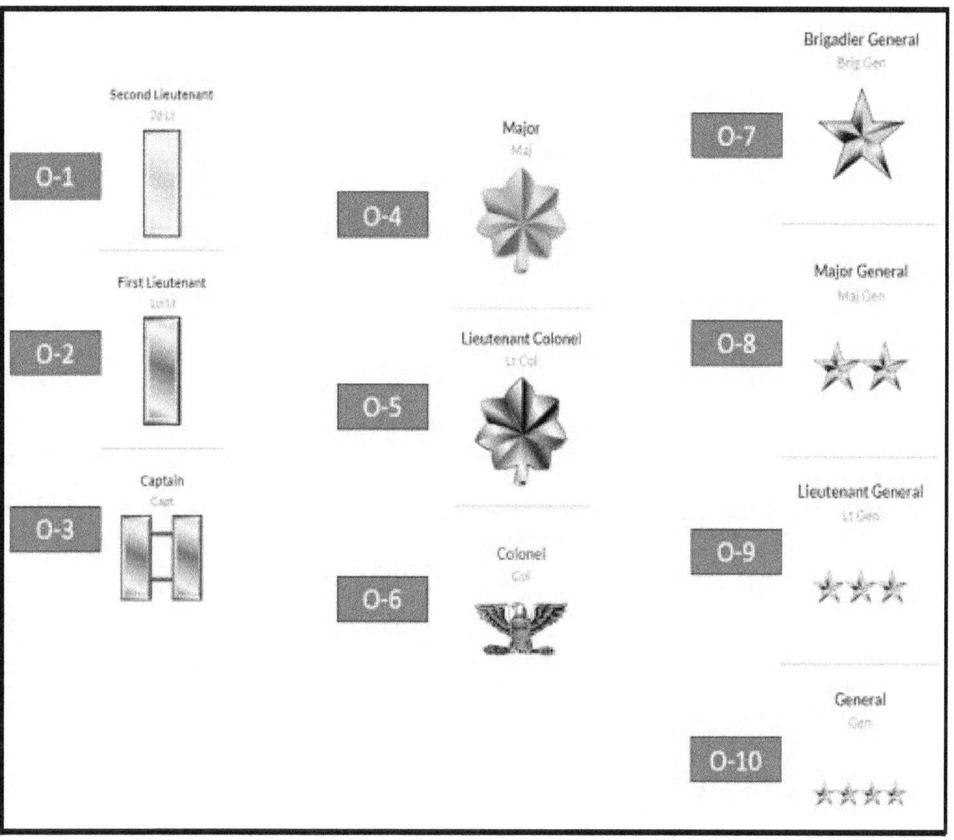

About the Author

Jose's journey began as an immigrant from Central America to the United States in his early childhood. From a young age, he had a fascination with the Air Force, a dream momentarily set aside but later rekindled as a promising opportunity. Fueling his childhood passion, Jose enlisted and embarked on a 20+ year career in the Air Force.

Growing up, he found solace and inspiration in books with quotes from celebrated leaders. He loved sharing those lessons with friends to help them in their life journey. This love for wisdom led him to compile his own treasure trove of lessons gleaned from other leaders he met along the way. In his book, 'Beyond the Ranks,' Jose shares these invaluable insights, offering a unique perspective forged through a lifetime of dedication and service.

www.ingramcontent.com/pod-product-compliance
Lightning Source LLC
Chambersburg PA
CBHW052009150726
47999CB00004B/1592